SHIBORI
DESIGNS & TECHNIQUES

To my husband Ian,
my daughter Jenny and
my sons Ben and Jack.

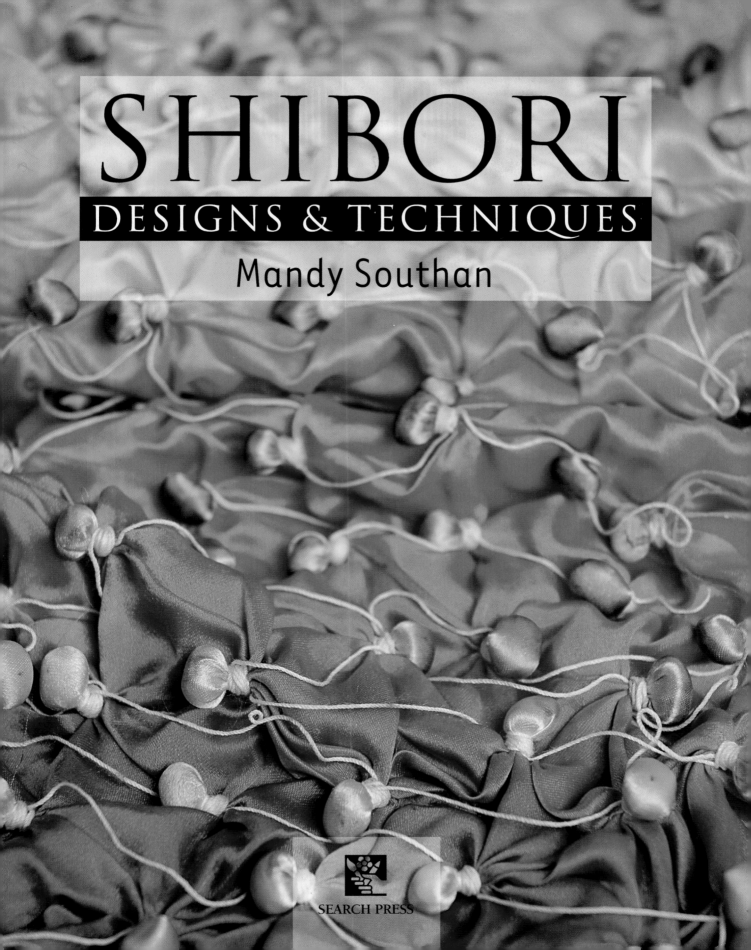

SHIBORI
DESIGNS & TECHNIQUES

Mandy Southan

SEARCH PRESS

First published in Great Britain 2008

Search Press Limited
Wellwood, North Farm Road,
Tunbridge Wells, Kent TN2 3DR

Reprinted 2009, 2010
Text and needlework designs copyright © Mandy Southan 2008

Photographs by Debbie Patterson at Search Press Studios
Photographs and design copyright © Search Press Ltd 2008

ISBN: 978-1-84448-269-6

The Publishers and author can accept no responsibility for any
consequences arising from the information, advice or instructions
given in this publication.

Readers are permitted to reproduce any of the designs in this book
for their personal use, or for the purposes of selling for charity,
free of charge and without the prior permission of the Publishers.
Any use of the designs for commercial purposes is not permitted
without the prior permission of the Publishers.

Suppliers

If you have difficulty in obtaining any of the materials and
equipment mentioned in this book, then please visit the Search
Press website for details of suppliers: www.searchpress.com

Publisher's note
All the step-by-step photographs in this book feature the
author, Mandy Southan, demonstrating shibori. No models
have been used.

Printed in Malaysia

Acknowledgements

*I would like to thank Yoshiko Iwamoto Wada — I am
indebted to her for the knowledge she has shared through her
teaching and her books.*

*Special thanks to Hiroshi Murase, shibori master, for
teaching me traditional Arimatsu stitching techniques and
to Kenichi Utsuki for showing me traditional shibori and
natural indigo dyeing while I was in Kyoto.*

*I would like to thank Caroline Munns of
Rainbow Silks for generously supplying the dyes and
materials for the making of this book.*

*Last but not least, thank you to my family for their
unfailing interest and support, especially my husband Ian
— patient and long-suffering as ever amid piles of samples
and buckets of dye.*

Contents

Introduction

*M*y first introduction to shibori was tie-dyeing in a bowl on the floor at school. I still remember the surprise and delight of undoing my piece and finding the cloth transformed into an extraordinary pattern. That pleasure has remained with me, and years later, I discovered that tie-dyeing was only one of many fascinating resist techniques that involve shaping and binding fabric before dyeing it. Tie-dyeing is one of the oldest methods of decorating cloth and spans a world of inventiveness stretching from South America, Africa and the Middle East across China, the Indian sub-continent (where it is called 'bandhani'), to Indonesia (where it is called 'plangi' and 'tritik') and Japan. It has been practised in Japan for over 1000 years and many ingenious methods have been devised to produce textiles of astounding beauty.

The Japanese term shibori, which means to wring, squeeze or press, now encompasses many different forms of tie-dyeing which all involve shaping and compressing fabric in some way before dyeing it. Fabric may be plucked and bound, stitched and gathered, folded and clamped, or wrapped around poles and pleated, and each method produces a different type of pattern. It works on the principle that dye can only partially penetrate into tightly compressed cloth and it creates subtle and intricate patterns within the folds. Water plays an important part in this process because it controls dye penetration (saturated fabric cannot absorb much dye) and acts as a medium for the dye to move in. You can never entirely control the process, so effects are often surprising and each piece of shibori is unique.

This book covers a range of shibori techniques. The majority are based on traditional Japanese methods and some are contemporary, or personal, adaptations. I have suggested a fabric for each project. You can experiment with different fabrics, as each will produce a different result, but make sure you are using the right type of dye for the fabric you are working with. The step-by-step projects show each technique from start to finish with variations showing the effects that can be achieved. By using a different fabric, or altering the shibori method or dyeing process, infinite variety can be achieved. When you have mastered a few techniques, try combining them to make unusual designs. I love the scrunchy, crumpled textures of shibori so seldom iron the finished pieces. Silk naturally tends to retain creases and this characteristic is exploited in Japanese shibori.

It is very satisfying to make your own fabrics. Japanese shibori techniques were developed for the narrow widths of kimono cloth and so are ideal for long scarves, cushion covers and other smaller items, but as you gain experience, you can make larger pieces.

The combination of ancient techniques and innovations using new fibres and processes now make shibori an exciting contemporary textile medium to work in. I hope this book will help you to discover its delights. Stitching or binding a piece of shibori is a relaxing and meditative process and watching dye transform the cloth is always exciting, but for me, the ultimate pleasure still remains in the moment of finally unwrapping the cloth to reveal the pattern.

Materials

Fabrics

Many different fabrics can be used for shibori and while some techniques work well on thicker fabrics, I have found the majority of shibori techniques work best on lightweight fabrics which allow the dyes to penetrate though several layers of cloth. Very fine fabrics such as chiffon and muslin can be folded into two or even four layers and worked together, speeding up the binding or stitching process. I have seen some very innovative shibori work using new fabrics such as heat mouldable polyester which can be used to create permanently pleated or crinkled, three-dimensional shibori textiles. Polyester is dyed with disperse dyes and can be heat set in a pressure cooker.

The fabrics used in this book are, from top to bottom: wool felt, silk/viscose velvet, silk habotai, silk satin, silk chiffon, silk crepe de Chine, silk georgette, lightweight wool, medium-weight cotton, cotton lawn, cotton voile, cotton muslin, wool and silks dyed with dischargeable black dye and silk scarves with pre-rolled edges.

Washing fabrics

Some fabrics are ready for dyeing, but generally it is necessary to wash your fabric before you dye it. Soak your fabric in warm water, then wash it in hot water with liquid detergent or silk wash to remove any grease or dressing, then dry and iron it ready to start your shibori.

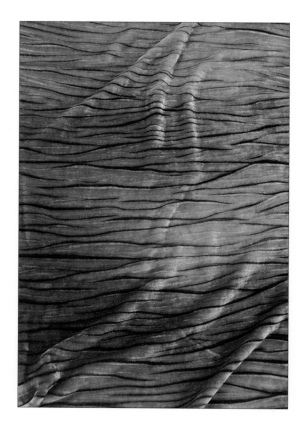

Silk/viscose velvet, dyed using the pole wrapping technique shown on pages 80–95.

Binding, stitching and capping items

A few inexpensive materials are all that are needed for binding and stitching projects. Binding and gathering are done with strong thread that will not snap under tension – a heavy cotton sewing thread is fine. String can also be used for binding. Elastic bands are useful items: small ones can be used for bean binding and securing short pole pieces, and large, thick ones can be used to clamp boards or secure larger pole-wrapped pieces. You will need a pair of small, pointed sewing scissors for tasks such as trimming threads and snipping knots on gathering threads. Alternatively, a quick unpick is useful for cutting knots. Long, fine millinery needles are best for the stitching techniques – you will need at least five so that several shapes or rows can be sewn at a time. A needle threader makes threading needles quick and easy. Cloth strips are needed for some stitching techniques such as mokume. The strips absorb the dye on the outer edges and avoid knot marks on the cloth. Dried beans such as mung, blackeye, soya and black beans are cheap and plentiful and are used in binding to stop the thread slipping. Do not leave your wet, bound fabric lying around too long though – the beans may swell or even sprout! Clay pastry balls can also be used for binding – they make slightly larger rings.

Thin polythene is used for capping. I save the thin supermarket bags used for fruit and vegetables, and cut them up. Corks from wine bottles are useful for plugging the space between the gathers in larger capped areas. It is a good idea to cover them with plastic food wrap to protect them from the dye.

Boards and clamps

Wood cut into pairs of square, triangular or rectangular shapes are used for board clamping. The wood must be fairly thick so it will not warp with the pressure of clamping and repeated immersion in dye and water. You can hammer short nails into the edges of the boards to wind string around to secure the folded cloth or you can use strong elastic bands or large jaw clamps (available in DIY stores) to clamp the boards. Small jaw clamps can be used to clamp lightweight folded fabrics without the use of boards. Line your boards with newspaper, cut to fit the boards, to protect your fabric from dye stains.

Fabrics dyed using the board clamping method shown on pages 66–67.

Poles

Different sizes of poles are used in pole winding and wrapping techniques. Short poles can be cut from pieces of plumbing pipe or sections of wooden broom handle. It is best to varnish wood or cover it with waterproof parcel tape to protect it from dye staining. Long poles can be made from metal stove piping (cover rough edges with waterproof parcel tape) or from PVC or polypropylene drain pipes and cable pipes. The longer the piece of fabric you are winding, the longer the pole you will need, and the greater the width of the fabric, the wider the diameter of the pole. Fabric is often folded down its length so that a smaller diameter pole can be used. Your limitation is, of course, the size of your dye pot. A deep bucket allows a fair length of pleated cloth to be dipped and you can also pour the dye with a jug over the pole-wrapped piece – lay it across a bowl to catch the drips.

Other materials

Cover your work surface with polythene and use a sponge to wipe up dye spills immediately to keep your surfaces clean – just a few grains of dye can spoil a beautiful piece of shibori work. Newspaper is used for steaming hand-painted silk. You will need a steam iron for ironing fabrics and finishing shibori pieces – you can steam them lightly, without pressing, to relax the folds without losing the texture. Use an old towel to squeeze excess moisture out of shibori pieces before dyeing, and pegs and a washing line to hang pieces up to dry. Kitchen paper is useful for wiping dye utensils and surfaces, and for testing hand-painted dye colours.

Designs drawn on paper can be laid under thin fabric for transferring, and moved to make a repeating pattern. Draw your designs on to your fabric with an autofade marker or a water-soluble pencil (test this first to make sure it washes out completely). Autofade marker ink dissolves in water but also fades automatically over a number of hours, so you will need to stitch or bind your piece fairly quickly. Card templates can also be used to draw around, and tracing paper is useful for copying designs and planning repeating patterns. You will need a ruler for measuring and marking out lines, a pencil and an eraser for drawing designs on paper (graphite pencil does not wash out of cloth) and a black pen for outlining a design on paper so you can see it through overlaid fabric.

Compasses are useful for marking out circles for karamatsu shibori. You will also need scissors for cutting fabric and card templates, and masking tape for sticking designs in place on the fabric and for securing steaming parcels.

Additional items include: a spray bottle for dampening shibori work; plastic food wrap for covering fabrics dyed with reactive dyes to prevent them drying out, and also for wrapping capping corks; waterproof parcel tape for sealing wooden poles and covering rough edges on cut pipes; and a kitchen timer for timing your steaming and discharging.

Safety

It is obviously very important to wear protective clothing when working with dyes and chemicals. Wear a plastic apron to protect your clothes and always wear rubber gloves – lightweight ones for preparing dyes and discharge chemicals, washing fabric etc.. and heavyweight ones for working with hot dyes. Always use a dust mask when working with powdered dyes and chemicals and wear a respirator and eye protection when working with discharge. Clean up with dye-removing hand cream – rub it over your hands and then rinse it off.

Health and safety when working with dyes and chemicals

Please note: reducing agents used for discharging are potentially hazardous and should be used and stored with care. Always store them in air-tight containers away from moisture.

Keep dyes and chemicals well away from children, pets and foodstuffs.

Always use, label and store dyes and chemicals according to the manufacturer's instructions.

Wear a particle face mask when working with powdered dyes and chemicals which can cause allergic respiratory reactions if inhaled.

Never use dyeing equipment or utensils for food preparation.

Do not eat, drink or smoke while working with dyes and chemicals.

Protect work surfaces and wipe up spills immediately.

Use clean, dry teaspoons for measuring dyes and chemicals and wash all equipment after use to avoid airborne particles.

Wear a respirator when working with discharge chemicals to protect yourself from fumes and work in a well-ventilated room.

Dispose of dye and discharge baths down the drain.

Dyeing

Dyes and auxiliaries

It is important to use the right dye for your fabric. Cellulose fibres such as cotton, linen and rayon can be dyed with reactive dyes and protein fibres such as silk and wool need acid dyes. You can use reactive dyes for silk but the colours will not be as strong. Most dyes dissolve easily in water but some stay grainy. A teaspoon of dye solvent helps.

Reactive dyes are easy to use and have good wash and light fastness. They need an alkali such as soda ash or washing soda to make them fix. Some reactive dyes require heat, but the easiest to use are the 'cold water' dyes. When using reactive dyes, it is important to measure the quantities carefully. If you use too much water, some of the dye will combine with the water instead of the fabric. Use them straight away – their ability to react diminishes within a few hours. Cooking salt (sodium chloride) is used with reactive dyes to help them dye evenly.

Acid dyes produce very brilliant colours on silk and wool and most have good light and wash fastness at lower temperatures. They need a mild acid like lemon juice to make them fix (you can use bottled lemon juice). Add about one tablespoon (15ml) to half a bucket of dye. Some acid dyes like black and turquoise need a slightly stronger acid in the dye bath. Use a teaspoon or two of citric acid crystals (from the chemist) to improve fixation.

Steam-fix silk painting dyes can be used for direct application methods on silk. They come in a wide range of liquid colours and can be intermixed and diluted with water to make tints. Silk painted with these dyes needs to be steamed over boiling water to fix it.

Discharge paste is used to bleach out dye. It can be bought ready mixed or as a liquid which is mixed with thickener to stop it spreading. Silk painting suppliers often sell discharge paste. **Discharge powder** (zinc formaldehyde sulfoxylate) is a powerful reducing agent used for discharge work on silk, wool and cotton. It can be added to water to make a discharge bath or dissolved in a little water and mixed with thickener to make a paste. Always use and store it with care according to the manufacturer's instructions – see the health and safety advice on page 11. Liquid or powdered illuminating dyes can be added to discharge paste to make a coloured discharge.

Liquid detergent (sold by dye suppliers) is very good for washing fabrics before dyeing and for removing surplus dye after dyeing to stop it re-staining the fabric. Use a small amount – it is very concentrated.

Equipment

You will need a large stainless steel bucket or stainless steel cooking pot (reserved only for dyeing) for dyeing large pieces. Small stainless steel bowls can be used to heat small quantities of acid dyes for samples or direct application. Enamel or plastic buckets or bowls can be used for cold water dyeing. Trivets such as pieces from a pressure cooker or a metal vegetable steaming basket are used to raise pieces above the water level when steaming.

You will need an electric ring or gas ring for heating acid dye and discharge baths and an electric kettle is useful for boiling up water for dissolving acid dyes and rinsing fabrics.

Kitchen scales are used for weighing fabric so you can estimate the quantity of dye and auxiliaries you need.

A plastic tray is very useful for catching drips when applying dyes by hand and for holding dyed pieces. A wire rack can be placed over the tray for direct application methods of dyeing and over a pot of boiling water for steaming. Foil is used to wrap around the pot and trap the steam.

If you are using the easy reactive dyeing method, you will need plastic bags to place your pieces in while they are fixing.

You will need plastic jugs or small bowls and a stirring stick for mixing dyes and a kitchen knife and 5ml teaspoons for measuring dye.

If you want to apply dyes directly, you will need foam brushes, paint brushes and plastic droppers or pipettes for applying the colours. Plastic palettes, ice cube trays or small plastic or glass pots can be used for mixing small quantities of colour for hand painting, and jam jars with lids are very useful for storing dye solutions.

A bent wire coat hanger is useful for twisting round short pole shibori pieces to lower them into hot dye or discharge baths.

Using acid dye

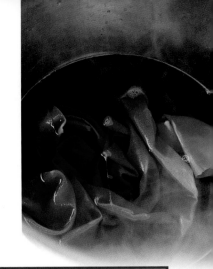

The beauty of dyeing shibori is that it is often not necessary or even desirable to get completely even colouration, and this simple dyeing method can be used. The water needs to be almost boiling to fix acid dye (do not actually boil silk as this damages the fibres). When you dye shibori, you often need the dye to 'strike' quickly and not penetrate too far into the folds. To dye silk shibori, soak the piece in hot water, then immerse it straight into the nearly boiling dye instead of raising the temperature slowly (the method which produces more even dyeing). Dye strengths vary and remember that dyed fabric looks much darker wet, so allow for this.

Measurements for dyeing 100g (3½oz) of dry fabric

Approx. 2 litres of water

1–2 teaspoons of lemon juice or 1–2 teaspoons of citric acid crystals

Pale shade – ⅛ flat teaspoon of dye	Medium shade – ¼ flat teaspoon of dye	Deep shade – ¾ flat teaspoon of dye	Black or navy blue – 1 heaped teaspoon of dye

1. Wash the fabric in a liquid silk detergent and rinse it well.

2. Put the fabric in a stainless steel bucket or saucepan with enough warm water to allow it to move freely.

3. Put the bucket on the heat while you mix your dye. Measure your dye into a jug with a teaspoon.

4. Add a little cold water and mix to a smooth paste.

5. Pour in a cupful of very hot water and stir well to dissolve the dye (check that there are no bits at the bottom).

6. Lift out the fabric and pour in the dye solution.

7. Add one or two teaspoons of lemon juice.

8. Stir well.

9. Immerse the fabric and stir continuously.

10. Gradually raise the temperature to 80°C (176°F), just below boiling point.

11. Maintain the temperature, stirring regularly until the shade you want is reached.

12. Lift the fabric out carefully into a bowl and rinse it several times to remove surplus dye, then wash it thoroughly in hot water with detergent. Rinse, spin or towel it dry and hang it up to dry.

Using cold water reactive dye

Measurements for dyeing 100g (3½oz)/approx. 1 square metre (39 square in) of lightweight cotton fabric

Use the same quantity of water, as shown, for each shade.

Pale shade – ½ flat teaspoon of dye, 6 heaped teaspoons of salt and 3 heaped teaspoons of soda ash

Medium shade – 2 flat teaspoons of dye, 12 heaped teaspoons of salt and 6 heaped teaspoons of soda ash

Deep shade – 4 flat teaspoons of dye, 18 heaped teaspoons of salt and 12 heaped teaspoons of soda ash

N.B. These are approximate dye quantities – some colours such as black will need more dye.

1. Place the pre-washed fabric in a bowl with one and a half litres of water.

2. Place twelve teaspoons of salt in one jug and two teaspoons of dye in another. Add half a litre of warm water to each of the jugs and stir well to dissolve.

3. Lift out the fabric, pour in the salt and dye solutions and stir well.

4. Open out the fabric and lower it into the dye bath. Stir and move it around to ensure the dye is taken up evenly. Shibori may be lifted and opened to allow dye to get into the folds. Stir every five minutes for twenty minutes.

5. Pour half a litre of warm water into a jug and sprinkle on six heaped teaspoons of soda ash. Stir it until it dissolves.

6. Lift out the fabric with the stirrer and pour in the soda ash solution.

7. Swill the jug around to release all of the soda ash solution into the bowl.

8. Put the fabric back and stir regularly for thirty to sixty minutes (longer immersion gives deeper colour and better fixation). Rinse the dyed fabric, then wash it in very hot water with liquid detergent to remove surplus dye. Spin or towel it dry and hang it up to finish drying.

Using reactive dye in a plastic bag

This is an easy way of dyeing small pieces of shibori.

Measurements for dyeing 100g (3½oz) cotton fabric (weighed before tying)		
Use the same quantity of water, as shown, for each shade.		
Pale shade – ¼ flat teaspoon of dye and ½ a flat teaspoon of soda ash	Medium shade – 1 flat teaspoon of dye and ¾ flat teaspoon of soda ash	Deep shade – 1½ rounded teaspoons of dye and 2 flat teaspoons of soda ash

When you are ready to dye, mix the two solutions together and use immediately as the dye reaction deteriorates over a period of one or two hours.

1. Dissolve one flat teaspoon of reactive dye in a jug with 100ml of cold water. Stir until dissolved.

2. In another jug, dissolve three-quarters of a flat teaspoon of soda ash in 50ml of warm water.

3. Pour both mixtures into a bowl, mix the two together and immerse your shibori fabric. Make sure it is fully saturated.

4. Take the piece out of the dye, squeeze it out, open it up and lay it in a plastic tray.

5. Loosely roll the piece up.

6. Place it in a plastic bag or cover it with plastic food wrap and leave it in the tray for one to two hours, turning it from time to time so it dyes evenly. Rinse it thoroughly in warm water, then wash it in very hot water with detergent to remove surplus dye. Spin or towel it dry and hang it up to dry completely before removing the bindings.

Direct application methods

You can hand paint, pour or inject dyes into the fabric to make multicoloured shibori pieces. When colours are laid alongside each other, they partially blend within the folds, creating surprising mixes and patterns.

If you are using reactive dyes, paint or pour your colours on and use the plastic bag method (page 17) for mixing and fixing your colours. If you do not want your colours to mix too much, leave the piece flat on a tray and cover it with plastic food wrap.

If you are working with steam-fix silk dyes or discharge methods, steam your fabric on a rack over boiling water to fix the dyes. Boiling acid dye can be poured over silk shibori using a heat-proof jug. Obviously, this must be done with care to avoid scalds. The fabric is laid across a bowl to catch the excess dye.

You can scrunch or hand pleat your fabric, then bind it with string, or put it in a net bag, as shown here, to keep it compressed. Different coloured dyes can be squirted or injected into the fabric using plastic droppers or syringes without needles.

1. You can brush the dyes on to your shibori. This piece of cotton lawn has been bound with clay balls and is being painted with red, yellow and green reactive dyes.

2. After fixing and washing, an attractive marbled effect is revealed when the bindings are undone.

You can place your piece on a wire rack in a tray to catch the drips. This piece of folded and clamped silk is being injected with magenta, violet and blue steam-fix dyes.

Steam fixing

Steaming is used to fix directly applied acid and silk painting dyes, and for some discharging techniques. Silk painters use upright or cooker-top steamers, which are ideal, but improvised steaming methods can be used, as shown below. Damp pieces can be covered directly with foil but dry pieces will be marked by condensation so it is best to wrap them in newspaper before covering them with foil. Wear rubber gloves when fitting the foil, to protect yourself from steam scalds. Steaming times vary – discharging may only take a few minutes, but a large piece of velvet will need at least two hours to allow the steam to penetrate fully. Keep an eye on the pot and top up with boiling water if necessary. Avoid water splashes or drips as these will mark unfixed fabric.

Steaming damp pieces on a wire rack

1. Place the dyed silk fabric on a rack over boiling water. This is a pole-wrapped piece.

2. Cover the saucepan, rack and fabric with foil and tuck it under securely so that the steam does not escape.

Steaming dry pieces on a wire rack

1. Unwrap and spread out your dry shibori on three layers of newspaper and roll it up as shown.

2. Fold the piece into a packet and secure it with masking tape. Steam it on a wire rack as shown on the left, for one to two hours, depending on the thickness.

Steaming on a long pole

1. Fill the bucket with water to just below the trivet top and bring the water to the boil. Stand the pole upright on the trivet.

2. Place foil over the top of the pole to trap the steam.

3. Cover the pole and the top of the bucket with foil and pinch it together to keep the steam in.

Note
Another method for steaming dry pieces on a long pole is shown on page 86.

Discharging on silk

Discharging adds a further dimension to your dyeing techniques and creates many exciting effects when combined with shibori. It is a method of bleaching out parts of a pre-dyed fabric to achieve light or coloured patterns on a dark background. You can discharge fabrics dyed with reactive dyes or acid dyes but only some dye colours will discharge completely to white. Some change to different colours depending on the dye constituents and some will not discharge at all, so buy dischargeable dyes or do your own tests, and be prepared for surprises.

The following demonstrations show discharging on silk. You can buy black dischargeable silk or dye it yourself.

Discharge agents are available in paste or powder form. They can be harmful so use them with care according to the manufacturer's health and safety instructions.

Note

You may need to adjust the quantities shown here depending on the product you are using. Do not be tempted to try household bleach – it dissolves silk!

Immersion method

1. Soak your piece of shibori thoroughly in water, then towel dry it.

2. Sprinkle one rounded teaspoon of discharge powder on to one litre of hot water, stir to dissolve it and bring it to near boiling point.

3. Place the shibori in the discharge solution. Here, a bent wire coat hanger is used to lower the pole-wound shibori into the solution.

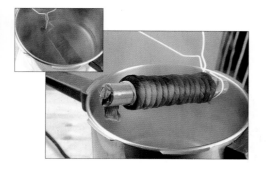

4. Hold the piece partially under the solution until you see the colour changing. Here, the pole-wound silk has turned red. Rinse it in cold water to stop the process and check the results.

5. You can dip again if you wish to discharge more colour. Here the silk is discharging to white.

6. Wash the piece in liquid detergent and rinse it well to remove the discharge chemical. You can either unwrap the piece and wash it straight away, or wash it on the pole, squeezing well, then rinse it and leave it on the pole to dry to retain the creases.

Opposite

Discharge tests on steam-fix silk dyes.

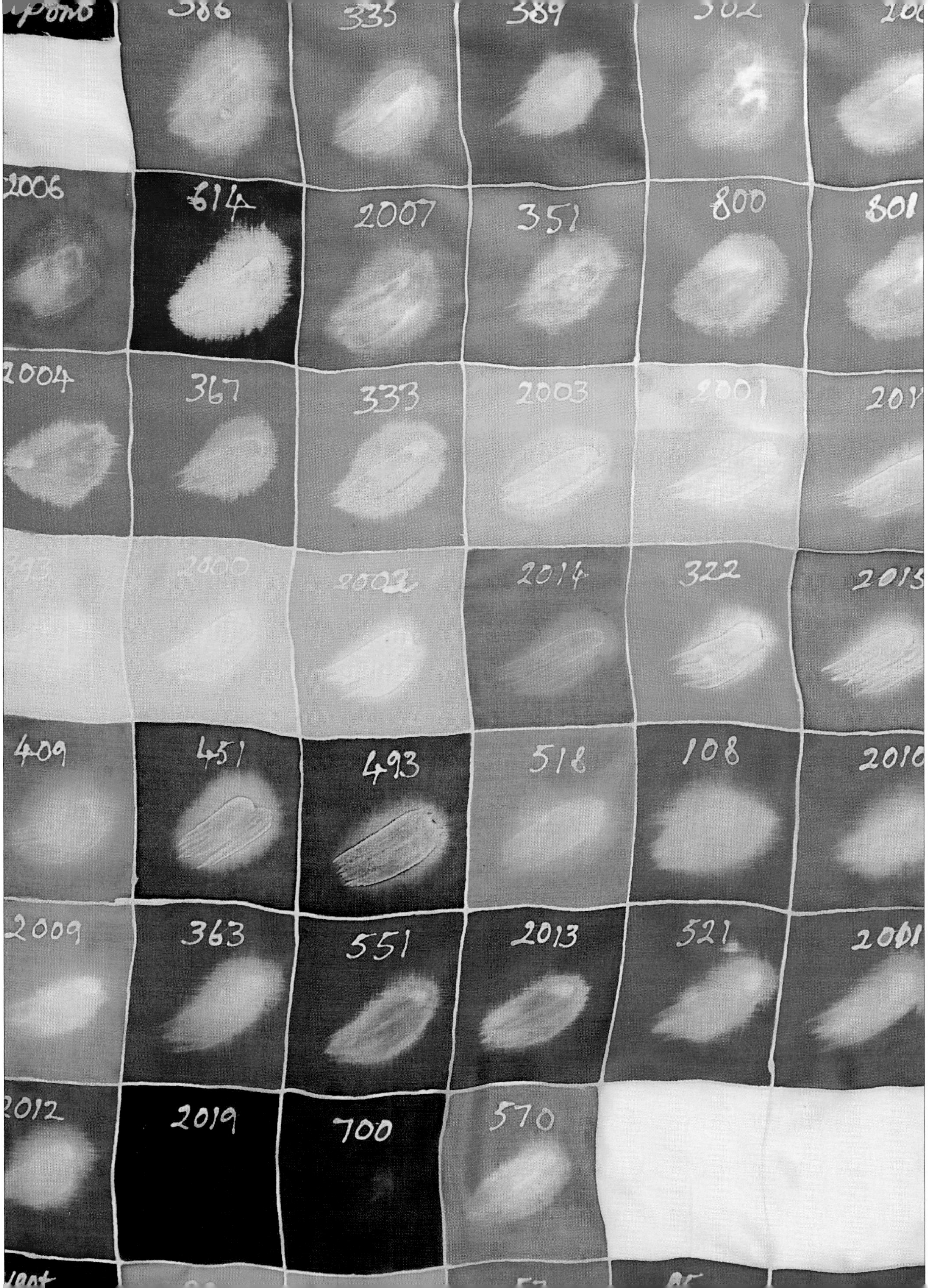
335
389
2006
614
2007
351
800
801
2004
367
333
2003
2001
2000
2014
322
409
451
493
518
108
2009
363
551
2013
521
2019
700
570

Over-dyeing

Shibori that has been discharged can be over-dyed with other colours by dip dyeing as shown here or by direct application methods. The discharge chemical often travels deeper into the folds than dye, so interesting haloes around the dye edges are created. Rinse your shibori thoroughly to remove the discharge chemical before dipping into the dye.

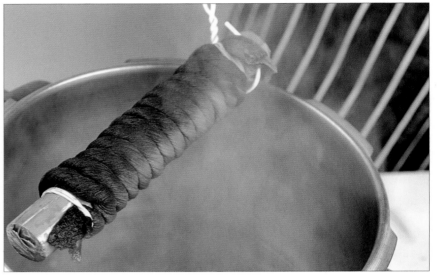

1. Dip all, or part of your damp, discharged shibori into dye. Here, pole-wound silk shibori is dipped into acid dye using a bent wire coat hanger.

2. Lift the shibori piece out, rinse it and check the colour. You can dip it into further colours if you like.

3. Rinse well and unwrap the piece.

Using discharge paste mixed with illuminating dyes

You can remove a colour and replace it with another colour simultaneously by using a discharge paste mixed with an illuminating dye. You can buy ready-mixed discharge pastes or you can prepare your own by mixing a liquid decolourant (or a small amount of discharge powder) with a thickener. Illuminating dyes are resistant to the discharge chemical and are sold in liquid and powder form. Liquid illuminants are easy to use and are shown in this demonstration.

Note

You may need to adjust the quantities shown here depending on the products you are using. Always follow the manufacturer's instructions.

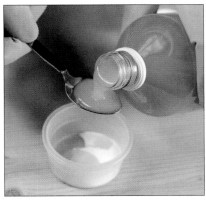

1. Mix one teaspoon of decolourant with three teaspoons of thickener to make a discharge paste. Mix well.

2. Add two teaspoons of liquid illuminating dye and mix well.

3. Apply the mixture to the damp silk with a brush, in stripes or dabs. The colours are barely visible at this stage – they appear when the silk is steamed.

4. You can apply a second colour mixture, with a little less thickener, by squirting it on to the silk from a plastic bottle.

5. Steam fix the piece as shown on page 19, checking every few minutes until the colours are bright. Remove the foil and rinse in cold water to stop the discharge process.

6. Unwrap the piece to reveal the pattern. Wash thoroughly to remove the discharge paste.

Space dyeing

You can dye 'rainbow' backgrounds for shibori work using space dyeing. Choose colours which are close to each other in the spectrum (see the colour wheel on page 27) for harmonious sequences. You will need several dye baths so you can dip from one to the next.

Note

It is a good idea to check your colours and tones before you start, by dipping little strips of fabric into the dye baths.

1. Mix three strong dye baths. Test each colour first on a spare piece of cloth. Gather up the silk in both hands and divide it into three as shown.

2. Hold two-thirds of the silk in one hand, leaving one-third hanging loosely.

3. Dip one-third of the silk into the first dye bath; here the turquoise, and stir.

4. Lift the silk out carefully and rinse the coloured part, still holding the rest in one hand to keep it undyed.

5. Hold the turquoise section and the other end section and dip the middle section into the second (blue) dye bath. Overlap with the turquoise slightly so that the colours blend.

6. Rinse the middle section only, holding the other two sections tightly in your hands. Dye the third section in the third, violet, dye bath, overlapping with the blue section to blend.

The finished piece.

Space-dyed silk georgette lengths, showing harmonious colour sequences.

25

Colour

Working with colour is part of the pleasure of shibori and some understanding of how colour is used in dyeing will aid your enjoyment.

Many dyers use colour shade cards and measure exact percentages of dye and auxiliaries for the weight of fabric so that they can reproduce exact shades. I tend to dye in a more intuitive, 'painterly' way – dipping and over-dyeing to get subtle shades and adding a bit more of this or that until I am satisfied. Admittedly, this takes some practice, but I do think it is important to enjoy the dyeing process and not get too bogged down in weighing and measuring. For this reason I have used teaspoon measures rather than grams or ounces.

I would suggest starting with a small range of colours as shown:

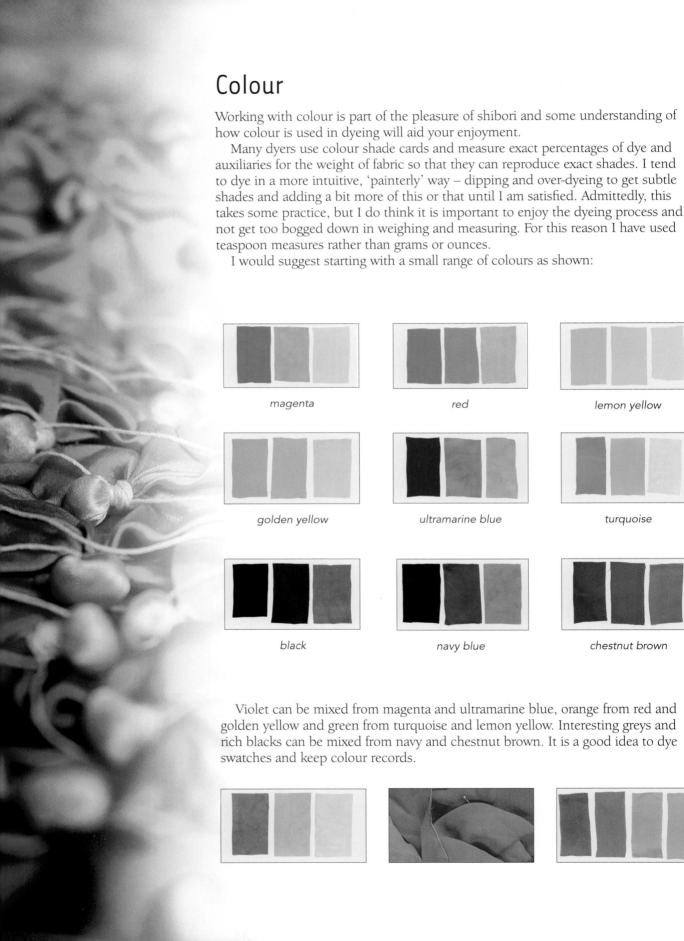

magenta

red

lemon yellow

golden yellow

ultramarine blue

turquoise

black

navy blue

chestnut brown

Violet can be mixed from magenta and ultramarine blue, orange from red and golden yellow and green from turquoise and lemon yellow. Interesting greys and rich blacks can be mixed from navy and chestnut brown. It is a good idea to dye swatches and keep colour records.

Dye colours tend to be rather unsubtle straight from the pot, so I usually mix them to make more interesting shades. It is not always easy to mix colours in the dye bath, however, because some dyes take more quickly than others: if a blue and a yellow are mixed in the dye bath, for instance, the yellow may be absorbed much more quickly than the blue and you do not get the green you expected. Over-dyeing (by dipping again in another colour) and direct application methods are often much more successful ways of mixing colours.

You can lighten the tone of a colour to make tints, by using less dye in proportion to the weight of the fabric. The colours on the opposite page are each shown with two tints. You will not go far wrong if you stick to tints and tones of the same colour while you are learning to dye.

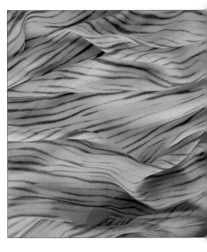

This pole-wrapped silk georgette was dyed in tones of the same blue.

The dyed fabrics on the right are arranged in a circle so you can see the sequence of the colours in the spectrum. Harmonious colours are close to each other in the circle, for instance blue/turquoise/green, or magenta/violet/blue. These colours work well in space dyeing and over-dyeing.

A harmonious sequence made by over-dyeing yellow with red to make orange.

If you mix or over-dye colours that lie opposite each other in the circle – red and green, orange and blue or yellow and violet for instance, much darker, more muted shades will result, as shown here.

Vibrant effects can be achieved by placing opposite (complementary) colours next to each other: see the pictures below of a piece shown in full on page 43.

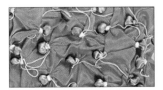

Unusual effects can also result when opposite colours partially blend, as shown in the piece on the right, in which violet and gold are used to suggest reflections in water.

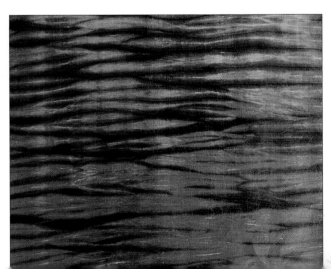

Binding

Binding is one of the simplest and oldest methods of decorating cloth. You can fold fine fabrics in half or even into four and bind several layers together to save time. Binding creates rings or stripes of different sizes. In Nigeria, cowrie shells or small pebbles are often used instead of beans. The size of the object will determine the size of the centre of your ring and the more times you wind the binding round, the wider your ring or stripe will be. You can use strong thread, string or raffia instead of elastic bands and you can bind your piece randomly or mark out a pattern of dots to guide you.

Simple Binding

This project uses mung beans and elastic bands to create rings in a lightweight cotton fabric.

> ### You will need
> White cotton lawn or voile
> Mung beans
> Small elastic bands
> Turquoise reactive dye

1. Place a mung bean under your fabric, pinch it in place and wind an elastic band around it tightly, without leaving gaps.

2. Continue binding the mung beans into the fabric.

3. Soak the fabric well then dye it with reactive dye using one of the methods shown on pages 16–17. Allow it to dry completely, then remove the elastic bands and beans to reveal the rings.

Two-Stage Binding

Rings and stripes of different colours can be made by binding and dyeing the fabric in stages. In this demonstration, yellow muslin has been used. You can buy this or dye it yourself with yellow reactive dye. You can also start your binding on white fabric so you have white rings too. The border stripes can be bound at any stage – in the demonstration they are bound over the yellow to make yellow bands and in the piece on the right they were bound at the red stage. You may find it easier to pleat the fabric for the stripes by spraying it with water to damp it.

Striped designs can also be made by rolling a narrow width of muslin into a long 'tube' and then binding it tightly in sections with string or thread. Indian turbans are often patterned in this way, binding and dip-dyeing several times to produce multicoloured stripes.

You will need

Yellow muslin
Large and small elastic bands
Soya beans
Red and black reactive dyes

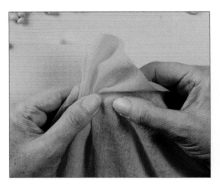

1. To create a striped border, finger pleat one end of the fabric.

2. Wind a large elastic band around several times tightly, to make a neat band. Arrange and pleat the fabric again a little further up and wind a second elastic band around it in the same way.

3. Bind in the soya beans tightly with the small elastic bands. Place them randomly, leaving spaces to add more after the first dyeing stage.

4. Soak the fabric well, then dye it with red reactive dye using one of the methods shown on pages 16–17. Wash and rinse it well then bind in more soya beans between the first ones.

5. Soak the fabric again, then dye it with strong, black reactive dye. Wash and rinse it well and hang it to dry before removing the elastic bands to reveal the yellow and red rings and the striped border.

Opposite

Another piece dyed using the two-stage binding method, but this time with the border stripes dyed at the red stage.

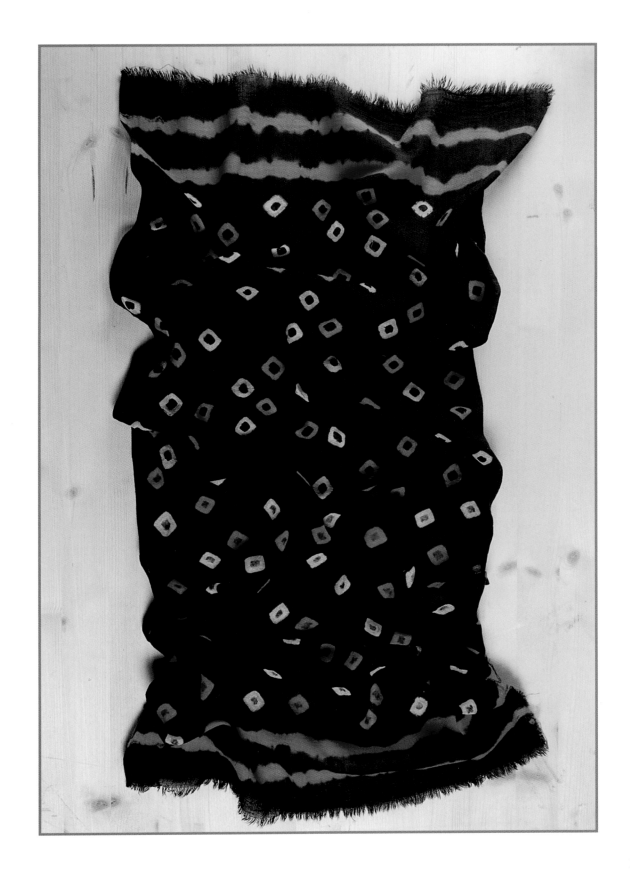

Binding Felt

Wool felt shrinks in the hot acid dye bath, making a permanently shaped, three-dimensional fabric. Some wool felt is a mixture of wool and viscose. This will dye with a two-tone effect. It is a good idea to test your dyes on your felt before you start. Hand-felted wool and wool felted with silk can be bound too, creating further possibilities for felt makers. You can dye the felt one colour or space dye it (as shown here) to create a shaded effect (turquoise changes to green on yellow felt). A pattern of dots can be marked on the felt to guide your binding.

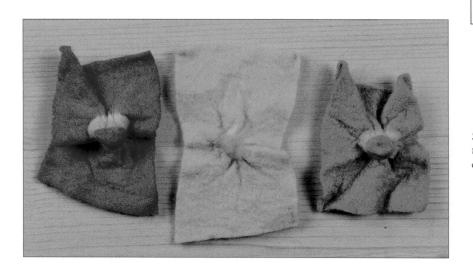

Samples of yellow felt, bound and dyed as tests.

1. Bind the mung beans into the felt with elastic bands.

32

2. Wash the piece and rinse it well, then space dye it by dipping the whole piece into pale turquoise and then one end into a deeper shade. Wait until it is completely dry before you remove the bindings to reveal the pattern and texture.

The finished piece, space dyed and retaining the shape of the bound beans.

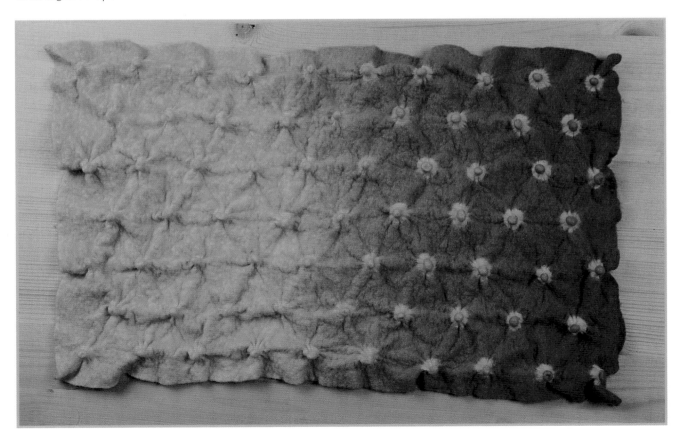

A variety of bound shibori felts in other colours and on hand-felted wool and silks.

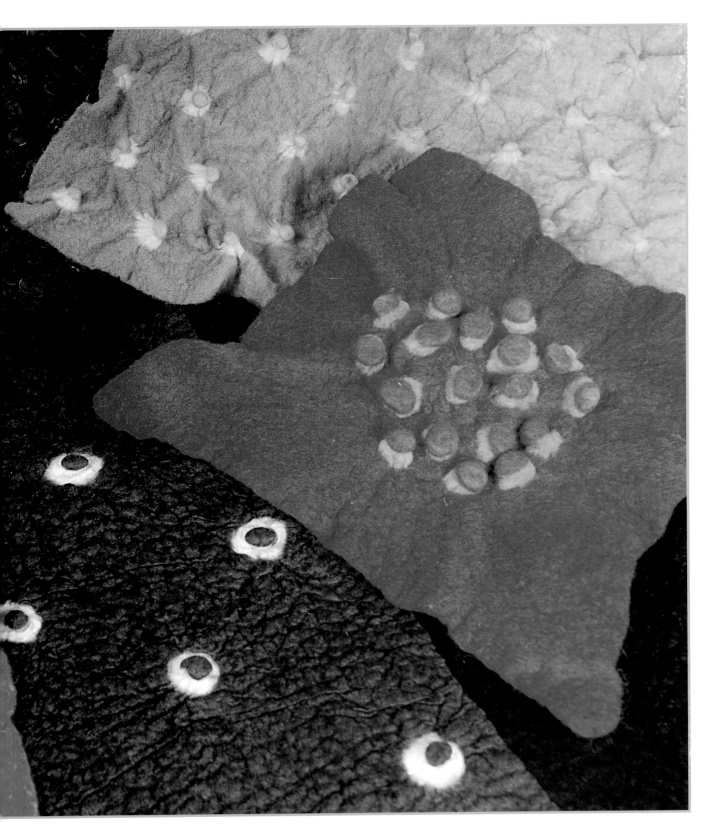

Spiderweb Binding

This is one of the oldest shibori techniques and variations of it, using a variety of binding materials, are found in many parts of the world. In Japan, it is called 'kumo' because the tightly bound, spiralling thread makes a pattern like a spiderweb and the tiny unbound portion at the end makes a dot in the centre like the spider. It is easier to pleat and bind the cloth tightly if it is damp. You can spray the cloth and the thread with water as you go.

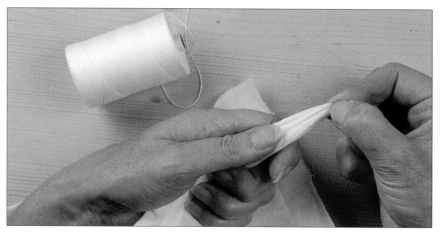

These bound pieces from Arimatsu, famous for its indigo-dyed cotton kumo shibori, show that binding is an art in itself!

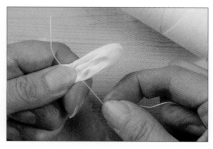

2. Take the end of the thread and hold it in place between your thumb and the pinched folds.

1. Pluck up a piece of fabric and keep it pinched firmly between your finger and thumb as you smooth down the folds neatly with the other hand. Pull the fabric taut, sort the folds evenly like a little closed umbrella and pinch them together firmly between your finger and thumb.

3. Wind the thread round the pinched section very tightly several times, trapping the loose end to prevent it from unravelling.

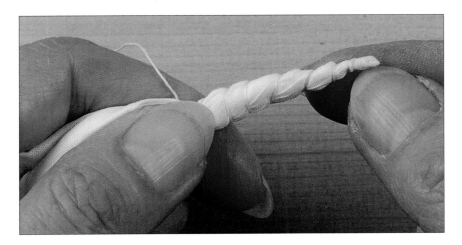

4. Pull the point of the 'umbrella' up and wind the thread tightly, round and round, as evenly as you can, spiralling up to the top.

5. Wind around the top a couple of times, then wind down to the base again. Secure with a kamosage knot (shown below). Do not cut the thread, just bind the next piece, following the steps again and continuing with the same thread.

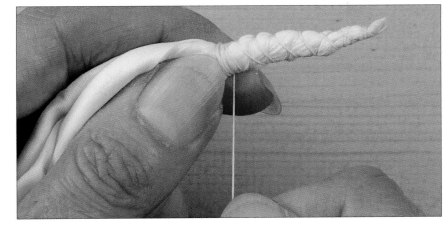

Tying a kamosage knot

A kamosage knot is used in many binding techniques. It is a simple twisted loop which holds firmly enough to secure the binding thread but is also easy to undo. The action is like making a simple casting-on stitch with one knitting needle.

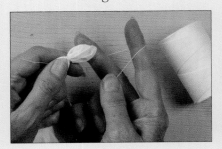

a. Make a loop with the thread around your first and middle fingers and hold the thread against your middle finger with your thumb as shown.

b. Turn your hand towards the fabric to twist the loop and poke the bound section through the back of the loop.

c. Pull the thread to tighten the loop.

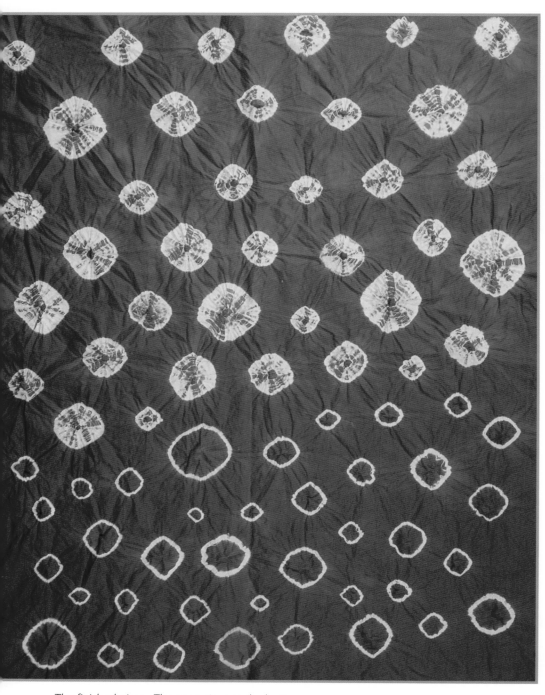

6. Soak the fabric well before dyeing it with red reactive dye. Wash and rinse it well. If you want to retain the creases, leave it bound until it is completely dry. You can unwind the bindings by pulling on the thread to release the knots.

The finished piece. The open rings at the bottom are made by simply binding and knotting around the base, without spiralling up.

Opposite
Further examples of spiderweb shibori on silk habotai and silk chiffon.

Kanoko Binding

Kanoko is a classic Japanese shibori technique used to pattern silk kimono and haori jackets. Silk retains the creases, giving the fabric a beautiful three-dimensional surface. There are a number of variations, depending on how the silk is folded and bound, which create tiny resisted rings, squares or rectangles. These may be arranged in lines to create patterns or repeated very close together to cover the entire ground, leaving spaces which form the design. It is the most intricate form of shibori and extremely time-consuming to do over large areas, but small designs are quite easy to achieve.

You will need

Silk habotai
Pencil and paper
Water-soluble pencil
Strong thread
Blue acid dye

Tip

Bind and dye a few test pieces before embarking on a large design.

1. Draw out a simple design.

2. Place the silk habotai over the design and mark out the dots with water-soluble pencil.

3. Pinch up the fabric on one of the dots to make a fold.

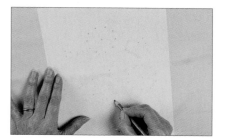

4. Fold the fabric into quarters, with the point of the folds on the dot, and then fold again into eighths to make a little pointed triangle.

5. Pinch the triangle between your left finger and thumb, with your thumbnail near the tip, and twist the tip anticlockwise with your right finger and thumbnail and flatten it.

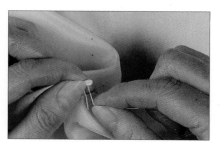

6. Pinch the end of the thread against the little twist and hold it in place with your thumbnail.

7. Wind the thread round tightly five or six times and finish with two kamosage knots. Do not cut the thread – take it over to the next dot to continue binding.

Tip
Hold the knot tightly with your thumbnail to prevent it from slipping off the end of the fabric as it is pulled tight.

Two of the dots bound with thread.

8. When the binding is complete, dip dye the piece briefly in blue acid dye.

9. Rinse and dry and then pull the silk on the cross grain to pop off the bindings.

10. Open the piece to reveal the pattern. Do not iron out the creases, which are part of the traditional effect.

Traditional Japanese kanoko shibori (the red shapes were capped – see page 47).

Tip
Japanese shibori artisans use a stand with a blunt needle to make a type of kanoko called 'tsukidashi', which is quicker to do. You can make an improvised blunt needle with a cut and bent wire coat hanger clamped to a table edge. Place your fabric over the 'spike' and position the dot. Pull the fabric down over the spike and hold it taut while you wind the thread two or three times round the tip. Lift the fabric off the tip of the spike, tighten the thread and make a couple of kamosage knots to secure it. Move the fabric across to the next dot and repeat.

Hand painting and capping

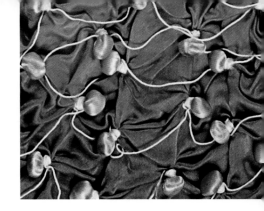

Capping is a technique which involves covering parts of a bound or stitched fabric with a waterproof material to protect it from the dye. Originally, natural materials were used for capping, but these days, polythene works very well. I use thin, soft plastic bags, cut up and folded in two, to ensure good protection. By hand painting and capping bound pieces, individual colours can be isolated from over-dyed colours. I like to use capping to enable me to place complementary (opposite) colours next to each other to create vibrant effects, as in this bean-bound project.

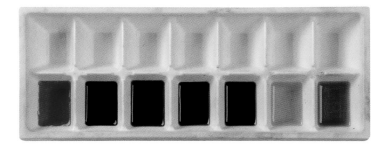

Silk paints in a palette. Greens can be mixed from lemon yellow and turquoise; greeny-blues from turquoise and ultramarine blue; and violet can be mixed from blue and magenta.

You will need

Silk satin

Tracing paper

Autofade marker

Blackeye beans

Strong thread

Steam-fix silk painting dyes in golden yellow, lemon yellow, turquoise, ultramarine blue and magenta

Palette

Paint brush

Polythene

Scissors

Acid dyes in violet, magenta, red and yellow

1. Mark out your design on tracing paper first and transfer it to your fabric using an autofade marker.

2. Use strong thread to bind in the blackeye beans where you have made your marks. Wind the thread around eight to ten times very tightly, then make a kamosage knot (see page 37). You can continue binding the beans without cutting the thread.

3. Use a paint brush to paint silk dyes on to the bound parts of the silk. Start with yellow at one end and progress through a rainbow of colours from green, turquoise and blue to purple at the other end. Leave to dry.

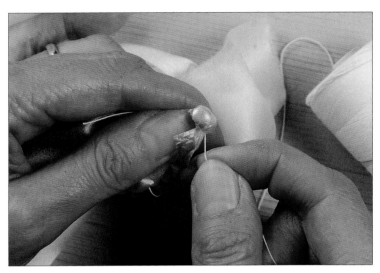

4. Cut little rectangles of polythene. Fold one in half, place it over a bound-in bean and use strong thread to bind the polythene in place in the same way as in step 2, finishing with a kamosage knot. Cap all the bound in beans in this way.

5. Space dye the piece in colours ranging from violet at one end (where the capped parts are yellow) through pink, red and orange to yellow at the other end, where the capped parts are purple. In this way the capped parts will be in complementary colours to the background silk, creating a striking contrast.

Note

The steamy heat of space dyeing is usually enough to fix the silk dyes on the capped beans. Test this by pressing a damp paper tissue on to the capped areas after space dyeing. If colour comes off, arrange the piece carefully on a rack and steam as shown on page 19.

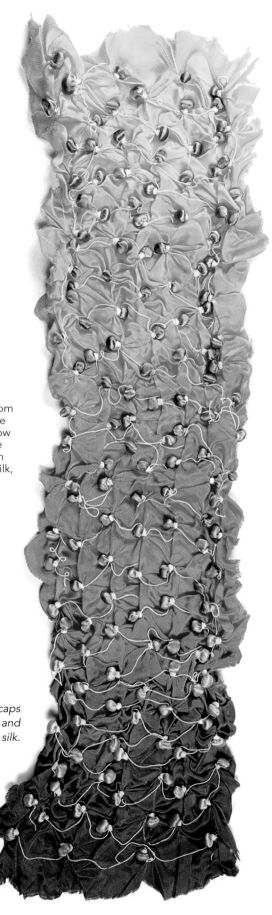

The rainbow-dyed piece with the caps and their binding threads removed and the beans left bound in the silk.

These hand-painted and capped pieces were bound without beans. The silk chiffon length was painted with circles of yellow and orange, then bound, capped and space dyed blue and turquoise. The rainbow scarf was bound in small sections, hand painted, capped and space dyed in complementary colours.

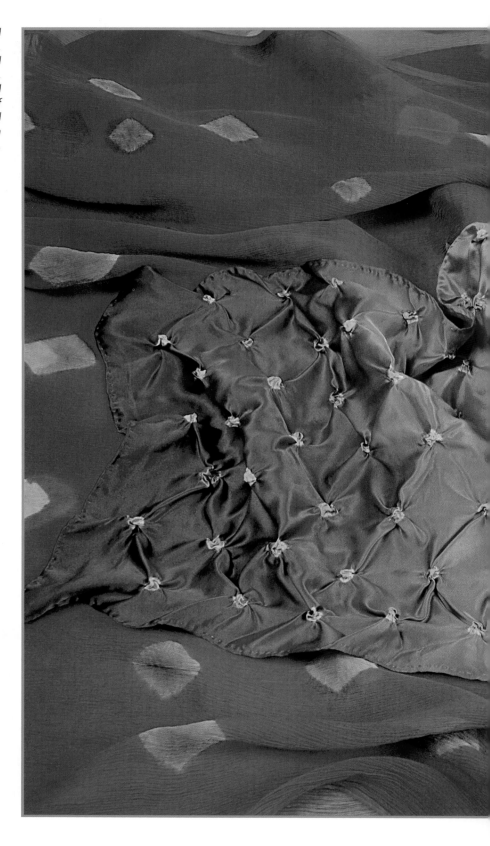

Stitching and capping

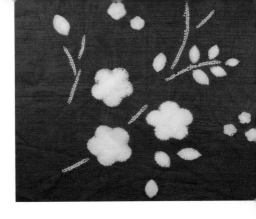

Shapes can be stitched and gathered and then bound with polythene to resist the dye. Small, simple shapes work best, as in this flower and leaf pattern. If your shapes are close together, it is easier to sew all the shapes first before pulling up the threads, as the folds in the fabric make it difficult to sew evenly. In 'tsujigahana', an old Japanese stitching and capping technique, the reserved shapes are painted and embroidered with delicate flowers and leaves, embellished with gold and silver leaf.

You will need

Cotton lawn

Autofade marker

Strong thread and needles

Needle threader

Polythene cut into rectangular strips

Quick unpick

Blue reactive dye

1. Draw some simple flower and leaf shapes like the ones shown on page 48, using an autofade marker.

2. Thread a needle with strong thread and knot the end. Sew round the outline of the shape in small running stitches, finishing just beyond the knot where you began, leaving no gap. Do not cut the thread yet.

3. Working with the right side of the fabric facing you, pull the thread to gather it carefully (you can put a fingertip inside larger shapes to prevent the folds getting trapped).

Tip

Larger shapes can be difficult to gather tightly enough to prevent the dye seeping in. Plug the space between the gathers with a piece of cork covered in plastic food wrap and draw the thread up tightly around it before capping.

4. Pull up the thread very tightly, then knot it by winding it around a needle (as shown on pages 50–51, steps 4, 5 and 6). Cut the thread. Repeat the stitching and gathering steps for all the flowers and leaves.

5. Cut a rectangle of polythene wider than the length of your gathered piece. Place it so the edge overlaps the gathering thread a little, as shown.

6. Wrap it tightly around the shape several times. Use strong thread to tightly bind the edge of the polythene round the base of the unit, trapping the end of the thread under the bindings to stop it slipping.

7. Wind the thread tightly from the base up to the top of your capped shape, turning down the end of the polythene as you bind, to seal it.

8. Bind tightly round the top and then down again and bind several times round the base of the motif before securing the thread with a couple of kamosage knots (see page 37). Cap all the motifs in the same way. Soak the fabric thoroughly in water before dyeing it with blue reactive dye. Hang it to dry before removing the capping and gathering stitches (use a quick unpick to carefully cut the knots).

The finished piece, dyed blue, with the capping and stitching threads removed and a variation, dyed green (below left). The stems are stitched using the ori nui technique shown on pages 50–51.

Symmetrical leaf shapes can be sewn by folding the fabric in half before stitching. These leaves and those shown opposite on silk crepe de Chine and cotton voile were gathered and hand painted (see page 18) before being capped and dyed.

Stitching and gathering

Ori Nui

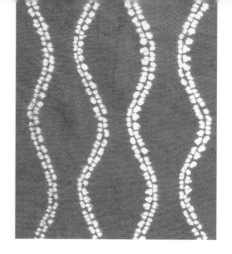

There are a number of different ways of stitching and gathering cloth to make straight or wavy lines. In this technique, called 'ori nui' (fold/stitch in Japanese), the fabric is stitched on the edge of a fold, to make a double line of dots. It is often worked diagonally across the cloth in wavy lines, but can also be stitched horizontally or vertically, and in short sections as in the stems on page 48.

You will need

Cotton lawn
Card template
Water-soluble pencil
Strong thread and needles
Needle threader
Green reactive dye mixed from
yellow and blue

1. Make a wavy line template from card. Use a water-soluble pencil to draw lightly along the template on your fabric. Move the template before drawing the next line to create a staggered effect as shown. Continue drawing wavy lines.

2. Thread five needles with long, double lengths of strong thread with good knots at the end. Working a short length at a time, fold and pinch the fabric along the wavy line and sew with a small running stitch very close to the edge of the fold through both layers of fabric. Do not gather the fabric at this stage.

3. Continue pinching and sewing along the full length of the piece and leave the needle attached. Sew four more rows in the same way. Pull the first thread to gather the first wavy line.

4. Arrange the gathers evenly, then pull very hard on the thread to compress the gathers tightly. Keep the thread tensioned and pinch the needle against the thread and fabric.

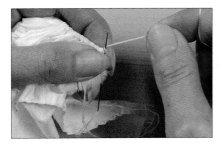

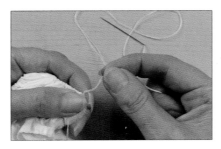

5. Wind the thread once or twice around the needle.

6. Keeping the tension and still pinching the fabric and the gathering thread, pull the needle through to make a knot right against the fabric.

7. Pull the knot tight, then repeat steps 4, 5 and 6, re-tensioning to make a second knot even closer to the fabric. Cut the thread. Gather and knot all the threads in the same way. Soak the fabric well and dye it with green reactive dye.

Tip

Sew about five wavy lines to start with, leaving all five needles attached. Gather the first line, then sew another line, and so on until all the lines are stitched and gathered ready for dyeing.

The finished piece, dyed green and ironed to reveal the stitching pattern. You can gently steam ori nui shibori to relax the gathers and still retain some of the texture, as shown in the orange and red pieces.

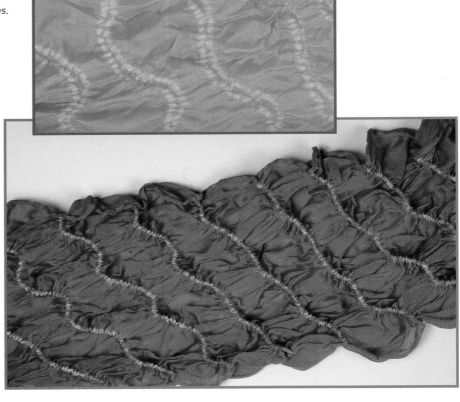

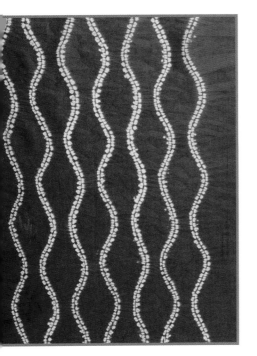

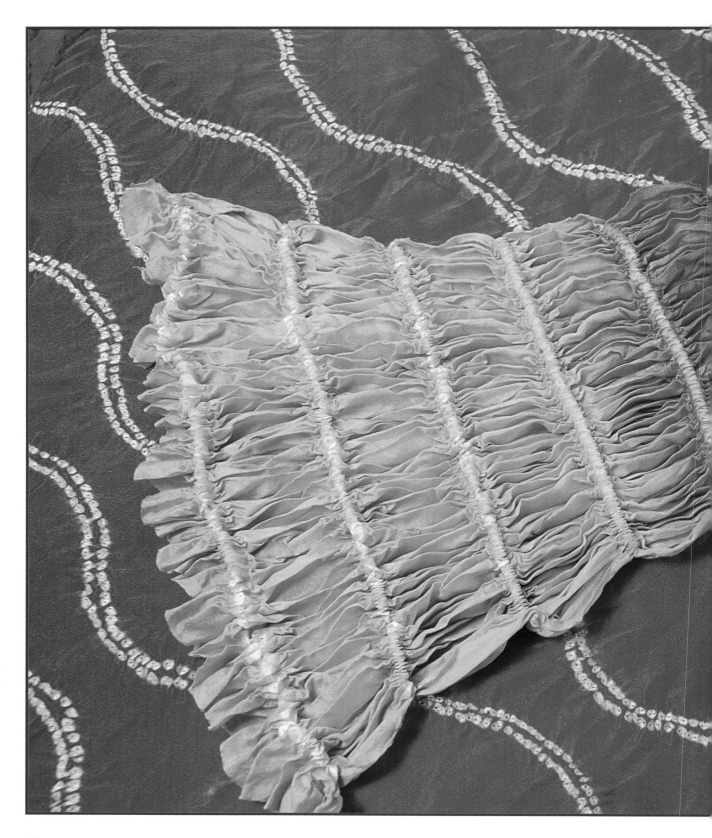

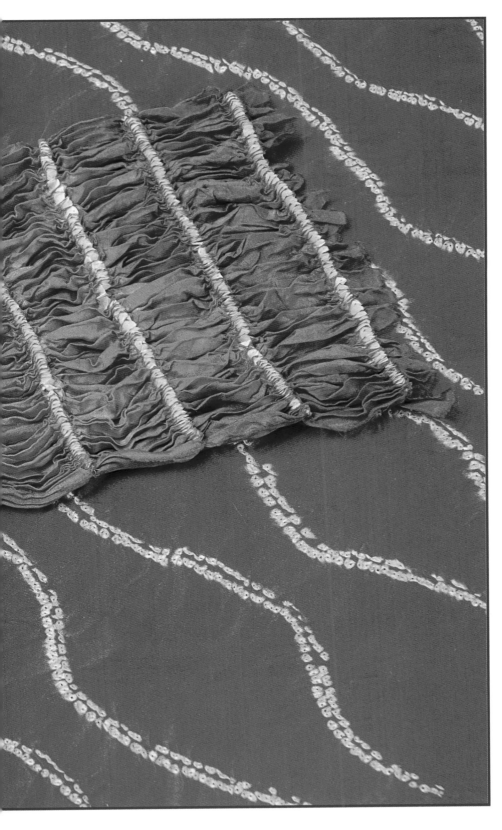

The red silk satin scarf was stitched diagonally across the width and ironed to reveal the pattern, and the silk habotai scarf was stitched in straight lines, then space dyed pink and yellow. The texture of the gathers makes an intriguing elastic textile.

Mokume

Mokume shibori creates lines and folds like sand patterns or tree bark (the word is Japanese for wood grain). It can be worked across the width of the fabric as shown here or used to fill in shapes. It is always worked in parallel rows set close to each other so the dye can not seep into the folds. Keep your stitches roughly the same length (the length varies depending on the thickness of the fabric) but do not try to line them up – the beauty of the technique is the way the lines break and reform. The trick is to compress the gathers very tightly – if you sew with a double thread you can pull really hard on the thread without snapping it. You can spray-damp the fabric to help compress it. Work with at least five needles so that you can stitch several rows before starting to gather; if the fabric is too bunched up it is difficult to stitch straight lines.

You will need

Silk crepe de Chine
Masking tape
Ruler
Water-soluble pencil or autofade marker
Cotton fabric strips
Strong thread and needles
Pointed scissors or a quick unpick
Black acid dye

1. Stick the fabric on your work surface with masking tape to keep it taut and straight. Mark dots 1cm (3/8in) apart using a water-soluble pencil and ruler.

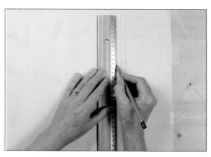

2. Using the dots as a guide, draw lines 1cm (3/8in) apart. Thread five needles with long, double lengths of strong thread with good knots at the ends.

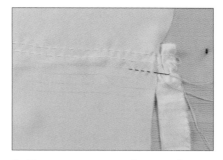

3. Place an extra strip of cotton along the edge of the fabric as shown to protect the outer edge of the fabric from the dye and from knot marks. Sew several stitches across the extra strip and then along the line in even running stitches.

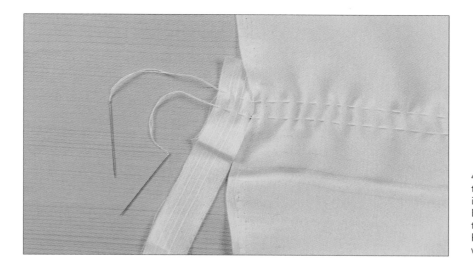

4. Place another strip of cotton along the other edge and sew a few stitches into this. Leave the needle attached. Repeat with the next needle and thread until you have sewn five rows. Remember not to line up your stitches with those in the previous row.

5. Gather up the first two rows you have sewn very tightly indeed, sorting the folds as you go, and knot the ends as shown in steps 5–7 on page 51. Then sew a few more rows and gather a few more alternately. It is best to leave a few rows ungathered above the line you are stitching, as this makes it easier to stitch a straight line. When the whole piece has been stitched and gathered, soak it well before dip-dyeing it in grey-black acid dye. Leave to dry completely, then carefully snip the knots and pull out the threads to reveal the pattern.

The finished piece, ironed, showing the distinctive mokume pattern.

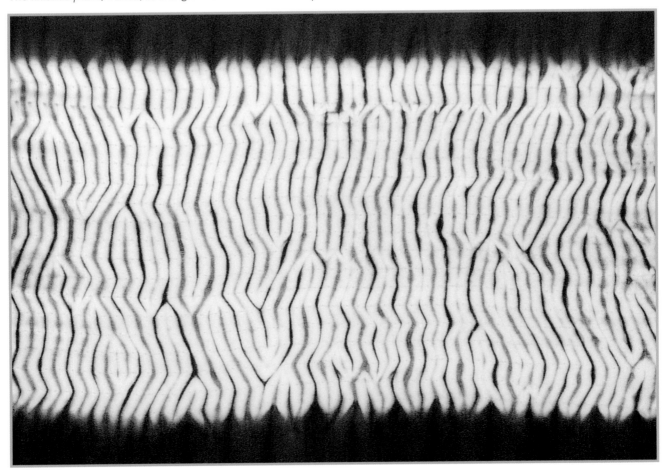

Mokume shibori on silk and cotton. Gentle steaming relaxes the pleats yet still retains the texture.

Opposite

Mokume borders, stitched and gathered, then injected with steam-fix dyes before dip-dyeing in navy and black.

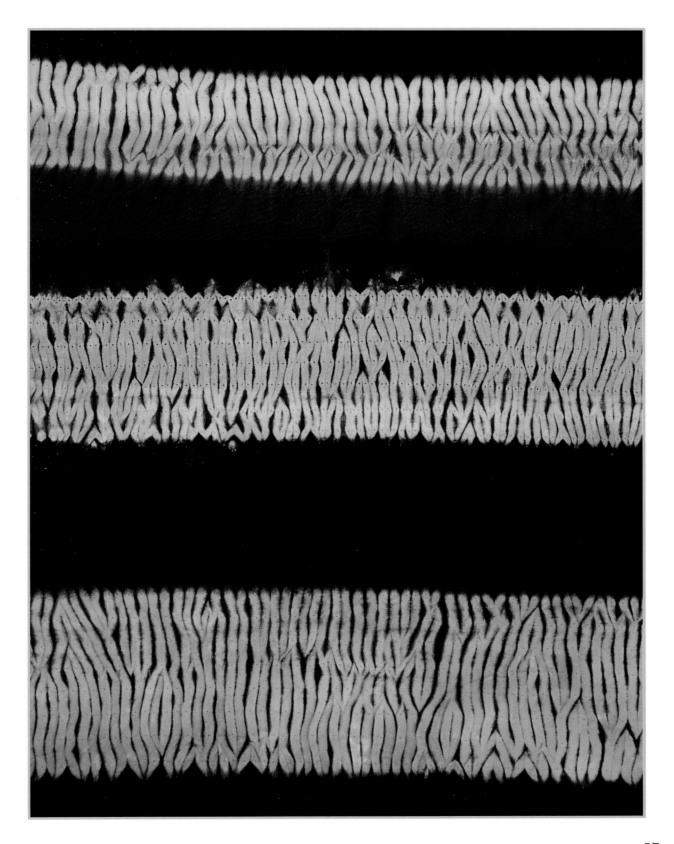

Karamatsu

Karamatsu, or Japanese larch, is an intriguing technique which creates circles with branching patterns radiating from the centre. You can stitch a single circle or a number of circles arranged in straight or staggered rows. This demonstration shows one line of circles being stitched and gathered. It is best to fold and mark out your whole piece of fabric before you start stitching. You can vary the number of stitching rows in each circle depending on how big you want your circles to be. The amount of space between each concentric circle will also alter the pattern – I would suggest you start with circles about 9.5cm (3¾in) in diameter and space the inner circles about 1.5cm (⅝in) apart. This project shows 9.5cm (3¾in) circles with three rows of stitching. The large circle on page 61 had twelve rows of stitching.

You will need

Silk habotai
Card and scissors
Compasses
Autofade marker
Strong thread and three needles
Blue acid dye

1. Use the compasses to make a circular card template. Fold the fabric and use the template to draw half-circles along the fold as shown, using the autofade marker.

2. Draw concentric half circles inside the first ones. I do this by eye, but you can make templates using compasses if you like.

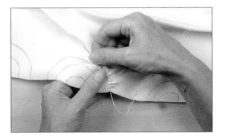

3. Thread up three needles with long, doubled strong thread and knot the ends. Make small running stitches around the first outer circle through both layers of fabric, then take the thread across and sew round the next outer circle.

4. Complete the outer circles, leaving the needles attached, then complete the inner circles in the same way. You can then add further rows of circles, staggering them to complete the design.

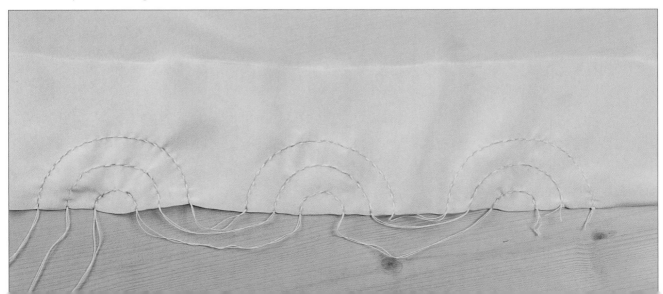

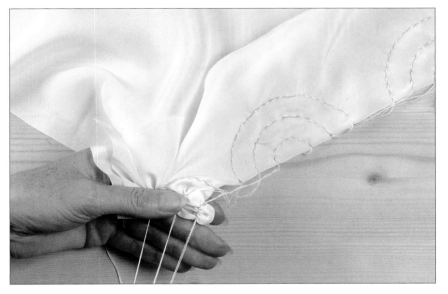

5. Grasp the three threads and begin pulling up to gather them.

6. Pull the threads tightly.

Note

You need the fabric to be flat so that you can stitch the circles neatly, so it is best to sew several rows of circles before you begin gathering, then stitch and gather the rows alternately.

7. Arrange the gathers evenly, pull each thread tightly and knot and trim it as shown in steps 5–7 on page 51. Soak the piece well before dip-dyeing in blue acid dye. Allow the fabric to dry completely before removing the threads if you want to retain the three-dimensional texture.

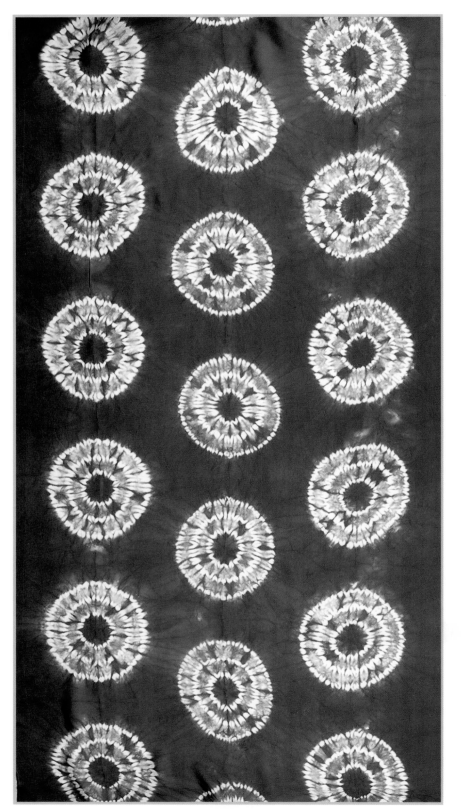

The finished piece of karamatsu shibori in a design of staggered circles.

Opposite

Examples of karamatsu shibori, ironed and left creased. The large circles were hand-painted with steam-fix silk dyes.

Folding and board clamping

'Itajime' is an umbrella term for a number of clamp-resist dyeing techniques used in Japan which produce symmetrical repeating patterns on fabric through folding and clamping. It is traditionally done with wooden boards bound with string as shown here, but you can experiment with pegs, paper clamps or other items which will compress the fabric tightly. The fabric can be folded into squares, rectangles or triangles to make different patterns. It is important to fold the fabric precisely to get an even pattern. Boards can be positioned in various ways to expose different parts of the folded fabric and infinite variations can be achieved by changing the size or shape of the board or clamp and by dipping the fabric in different ways.

Square folding

1. Cut the fabric to four times the width of the boards you will be using. Fold it in half lengthwise and iron it, lining up the edges carefully.

2. Fold over one half lengthwise, concertina style, making sure the edges are lined up.

You will need

Cotton lawn

Iron

Two square wooden boards with a nail hammered into the middle of each side

String

Newspaper squares to fit the boards

Blue reactive dye

3. Fold over the other half lengthwise, concertina style and iron the whole length again.

4. Fold over the end of the fabric to the size of the square boards you will be using.

5. Turn the whole piece over and fold the square end back on itself.

6. Continue folding back and forth, keeping the edges aligned until you have a pile as shown.

7. Cover each board with a square of newspaper to protect the fabric from the dye in the wood.

8. Place the fabric pile between the boards and newspaper squares. Tap the sides with your palms to line up the edges carefully.

9. Press down hard on the boards to compress the fabric. Wind the string around a nail on the upper board and then around a lower nail, keeping it tensioned and leaving a tail of string for tying later.

10. Wind back round the top nail, then take the string over the board to the other side and wind it tightly around the opposite nails in the same way, keeping the fabric tightly compressed. Go across the corner and begin to work on the next side. Press down hard to maintain the tension.

11. Repeat with the other two sides and then tie the string in a bow with the tail you left.

12. Soak the clamped fabric in water, weighing it down to keep it under the water, until no more bubbles rise. Loosen the string and press down hard to further compress the wet fabric, then re-tie the string tightly.

13. Prepare a strong dye bath and carefully dip one side so that the edges dip just below the surface. Hold it in until the desired shade is reached and repeat for the other three sides.

14. Use the plastic bag method to fix the reactive dye for several hours, then rinse the fabric, still between the boards, then untie the string.

15. Unfold the fabric to reveal the square pattern. Wash well to remove surplus dye.

Square-folded and board-clamped pieces. The square pattern varies, depending on how deeply the edges are dipped.

Triangular folding

This demonstration shows the basic triangular folding method and the pattern created by dyeing the edges only. Triangular folding creates many variations of star- and hexagon-shaped patterns depending on how the block is dipped. Fabrics that are more difficult to fold neatly can be sprayed and ironed with each fold, as shown here.

You will need

Cotton lawn

Iron

Two triangular wooden boards with a nail hammered into the middle of each side

String

Newspaper squares to fit the boards

Blue reactive dye

1. Fold the length of fabric into four, concertina-wise, lining up the edges carefully and ironing. Fold back the corner 45°.

2. Spray the fabric with water and iron again.

3. Turn the fabric over, spray and iron again.

4. Fold the fabric over at the angle shown to create a triangle shape.

5. Fold the fabric over the edge of the triangle again as shown. Neatly line up the edges, spray and iron each time you make a fold.

6. Continue to fold back and forth concertina-wise until you have a neat triangular pile of fabric as shown.

7. Clamp, soak and dye the fabric as on page 63, then undo the string.

8. Unfold the fabric to reveal the pattern. Wash it well to remove surplus dye.

Triangular folding on cotton and silk.

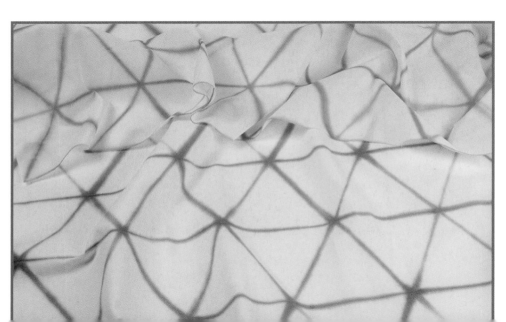

Sekka

Sekka means 'folded flower' or 'snowflake'. It is a traditional Japanese technique, often done on cotton dyed with indigo, but it also works well on silks and fine woollen fabrics dyed with acid dyes. Two corners are dipped to make flower shapes in a hexagon pattern. Silk chiffon and other fine fabrics, which fold to a thin pile, can be held with a jaw clamp and rectangular boards can be used to expose more fabric to the dye. The fabric can be folded and sprayed with water to help to compress it.

You will need

Silk chiffon
Iron and spray bottle
Rectangular boards and jaw clamp
Navy blue acid dye

1. Fold the fabric as shown on page 65. Place the piece between two rectangular boards as shown. You can cover the boards in plastic food wrap to protect them from dye if you want to.

2. Hold the boards together with a clamp. Immerse the piece in water for ten minutes.

3. Dip a corner into navy blue dye.

4. Rinse the dyed corner, then carefully move the clamp and boards to expose a second corner and dip dye this in the same way. Only dye two corners. Rinse and remove the clamp. Unfold and wash the fabric.

Tip

Different shaped boards can be used to expose more or less of the fabric to the dye.

Dyeing an edge using rectangular boards held in a jaw clamp.

Dyeing an edge using triangular boards held in a jaw clamp.

The finished piece.

Sekka shibori on silk chiffon and fine wool dipped in navy,
and cotton lawn dipped into more than one colour.

Folding and clamping with direct dyeing

Intricate, colourful designs reminiscent of kaleidoscope patterns can be created on fine silk by injecting dye into a folded and clamped piece. Different clamps can be used – these small jaw clamps are surprisingly effective; the little square ends of the clamps resist the dye and make a pattern of white marks. Steam-fix dyes work well for this technique and blend in the folds to create surprisingly complex patterns.

1. Fold the silk chiffon as shown on page 65 and clamp the pile in two places with small jaw clamps.

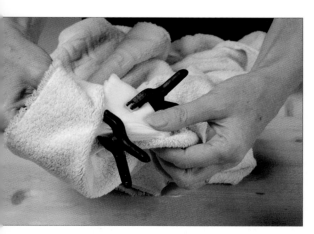

2. Soak the fabric thoroughly and squeeze out excess water with a towel by pinching carefully.

3. Use two steam-fix dyes: ultramarine and magenta. Fill palette wells with concentrated and diluted colours, some mixed.

4. Arrange the folds and points carefully and place the piece on a rack in the plastic tray. Inject dye into the fabric using droppers. Use the lighter colours first.

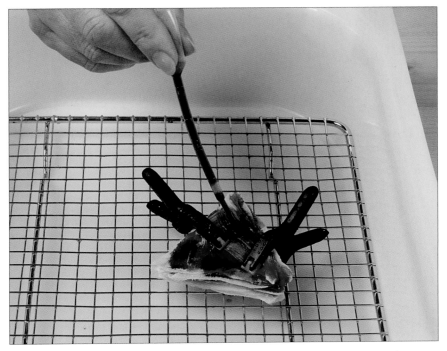

5. Add more colours, using a different dropper for each colour and pushing the droppers into the fabric as you squirt in the dye.

6. Check the other side of the piece to make sure the colours are penetrating and add more dye this side if necessary until all, or most, of the white silk is coloured. Do not move the clamps. Lift the rack, place it over boiling water and cover it with foil (see page 19). Steam it for twenty minutes. Rinse and unwrap.

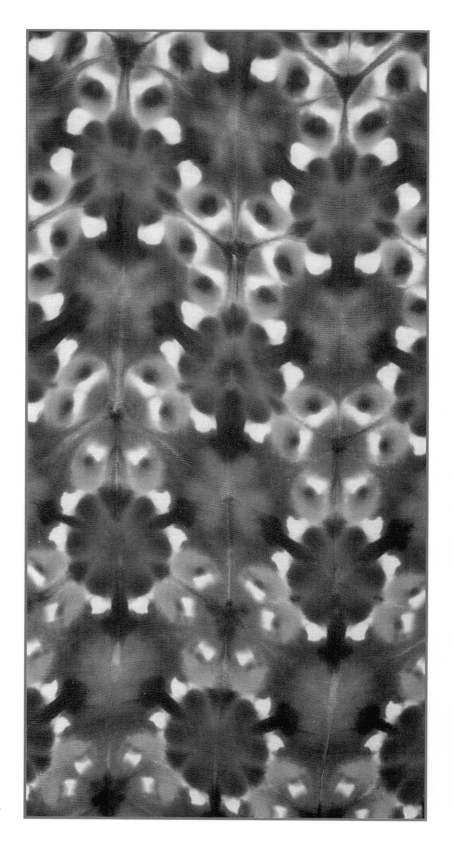

The finished piece.

Clamped and dye-injected silk chiffons. Infinite variations in pattern occur.
The piece on the right was also discharged with blue illuminant (see page 23).

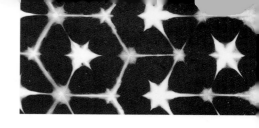

Folding and board clamping with discharging

You can get some surprising effects when you discharge board-clamped pieces. This technique works well on a range of silks and also on fine woollen fabrics. You can dye your own fabrics with dischargeable acid dyes or buy black dischargeable silk. You can discharge alone (haloes of lighter colours often appear round the edges) or rinse and then over-dye with other colours, keeping the boards in place. This demonstration shows a different way of clamping your boards using strong elastic bands.

You will need

Black dischargeable silk
Boards and rubber bands
Discharge solution

1. Triangle fold the black fabric (see page 65) and clamp it between two boards held together with elastic bands. Soak well to saturate it and dip one corner into heated discharge solution (see page 20).

2. Rinse and check to see how far the discharge has penetrated. Dip again if necessary.

3. Keep the clamps in place and dip the black edge just below the surface. Rinse and check for penetration again. Wash well with liquid detergent, rinse and iron damp to remove the creases.

The finished folded, clamped and discharged piece.

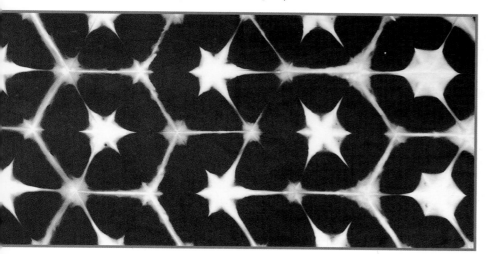

Opposite

Clamped and discharged silk habotai, silk chiffon and fine wool scarves. The multicoloured pieces were over-dyed by dipping the clamped fabric into different coloured dye baths.

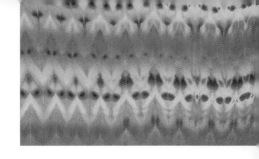

Pole winding

Short pole winding and direct dyeing

This simple method of twisting and winding a length of fabric on to a short pole produces complex bands of intricate pattern. It works best on fine silks like chiffon and georgette and is ideal for scarves 40cm (15¾in) wide x 152cm (60in) long. Every piece comes out differently depending on the colours you use and how you apply them. The simplest method for folding the fabric is demonstrated here. More regular patterns are achieved by folding the silk concertina-wise. If you want to retain the texture, wash the silk on the pole and let it dry completely before unwinding it.

You will need

Silk georgette 40cm (15¾in) wide

Iron

Short wooden pole, around 20cm (8in) long, wrapped in parcel tape

Two elastic bands

Plastic tray and wire rack

Steam-fix silk painting dyes

Plastic droppers and palette

1. Iron the silk georgette. Fold it in half lengthwise, line up the edges carefully and iron the fold.

2. Fold the piece in half lengthwise again, folding from the folded edge downwards. Iron again.

3. Fold in half lengthwise again and iron.

4. Continue folding and ironing until the piece is about 1.5 cm (⅝in) wide.

5. Wind an elastic band round each end of your pole. Tuck one end of your folded piece under one elastic band so it is held firmly.

6. Hold the pole in your left hand and the folded strip in your right and wind the pole clockwise around the strip so that the strip twists into a tight cord as it winds on to the pole. (If you are left-handed, reverse the instructions.)

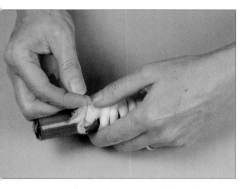

7. Continue winding, pushing the fabric down the pole as you go. Secure the other end under the elastic band, holding the silk firmly with your left thumb to prevent it from unravelling.

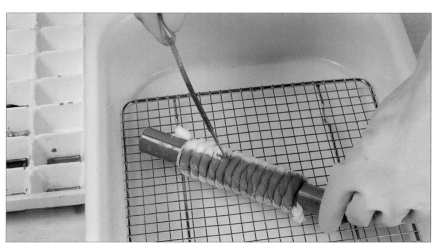

8. Soak the piece in water for ten minutes until it is saturated. Squeeze it in a towel and place it on a wire rack in a plastic tray. In a palette, mix magenta and golden yellow dyes in various concentrations to obtain different shades. Inject the dyes into the wound silk in bands, using droppers. Use different droppers for different colours.

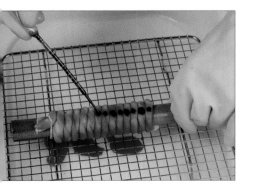

9. Add undiluted dots of ultramarine dye. Turn the pole and add more.

10. Leave the piece for ten minutes to allow the colours to soak in. Lift the rack on top of the steamer and cover it with foil. Steam for twenty minutes and rinse under cold water.

11. Unwind the fabric and open it out to reveal the pattern. Wash it in warm soapy water, rinse and spin it, then hang it out to dry.

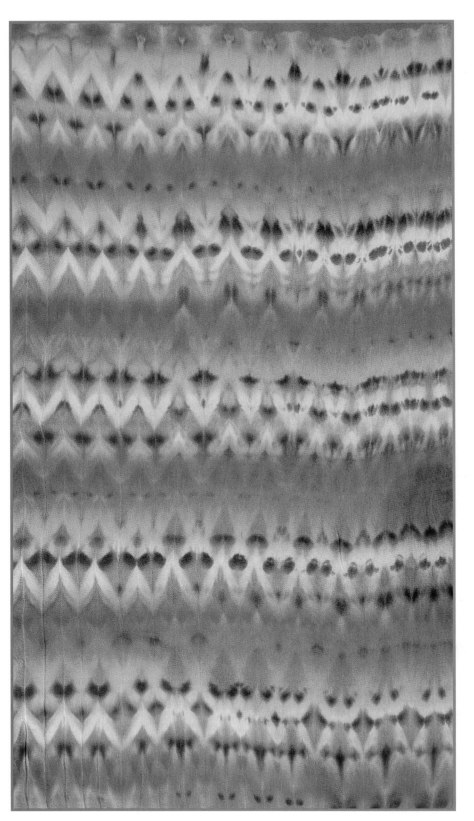

Opposite

Pole-wound silks showing the intricate patterns that form as the dyes merge in the twisted folds.

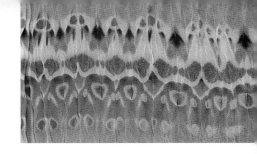

Short pole winding, dyeing and discharging

You can take the last project a step further by discharging and illuminating parts of your pole-dyed fabric. This creates more defined patterns, and exciting colour combinations can be achieved without the colours mixing.

You will need

Dyed piece from previous project

Discharge paste with blue illuminant

Paint brush

Plastic tray and rack

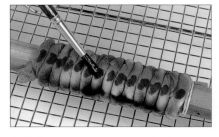

1. Follow the same steps as in the previous project (pages 74–75), but do not unwind the piece. After steam fixing, place the piece on a rack in a plastic tray and apply discharge paste mixed with an illuminant, using a brush. Dab on the mixture in three rows.

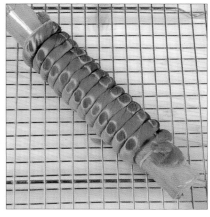

2. Place the rack on a steamer, cover with foil and steam (as shown on page 19). Rinse thoroughly. Steaming brings out the colour as shown.

3. Unwind the piece to reveal the pattern. Wash it thoroughly in warm water with silk detergent to remove the discharge paste.

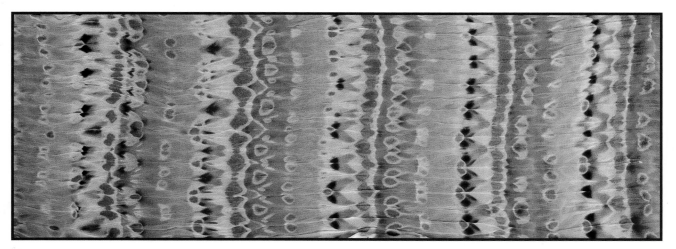

The finished piece.

Opposite
Pole wound and discharged silks.

Pole wrapping

Short pole wrapping with discharging

This technique can be done on a short length of broom handle or a piece of plumbing pipe. The diameter of the pole will alter the pattern and larger poles allow you to wrap wider widths of silk. You can wrap a surprisingly long piece on a short pole by winding and pushing up the silk in stages. Discharging black pole-wrapped silk with illuminating colours creates attractive zigzag patterns on a dark background.

You will need

40cm (15¾in) wide silk chiffon dyed with dischargeable black acid dye

Iron

Short pole, approx. 26cm (10¼in) long

Two elastic bands

Discharge paste with pink, yellow and blue illuminants

Paint brush

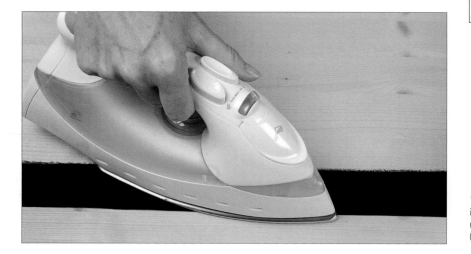

1. Fold the silk in half lengthwise and iron it. Fold again lengthwise, iron and repeat until you have a strip about 5cm (2in) wide.

2. Wind an elastic band round each end of your pole. Tuck one corner of the folded piece under one of the elastic bands at an angle of 45°.

3. Wrap the piece round the pole as shown. Butt the edges up against each other but do not overlap them.

4. Hold the fabric to keep it closely wound and push it hard along the pole to compress it.

5. Continue wrapping and pushing up the fabric. Tuck the end under the other elastic band to secure the fabric. Apply illuminants mixed with discharge paste, leaving space between the stripes to retain some black. Steam as before, checking every few minutes to see how the effect is going. When the colours are bright enough, rinse well in cold water to stop the discharge. You can dry the piece on the pole and then unwrap it to retain the creases.

81

The finished piece.

Pole-wrapped and
discharged silk chiffon.

Pole wrapping silk velvet

This method of pole wrapping pleats the fabric unevenly, creating wave-like patterns. It works particularly well on silk velvet hand-painted with steam-fix silk dyes. These dyes generally dye silk/viscose velvet well, but test your own dyes before embarking on a large piece. Pleated velvet takes a long time to dry, so put it in a warm place and be prepared to wait up to two days before unwrapping it. This method of compressing a tube of fabric on a pole is based on a Japanese technique called 'bomaki'.

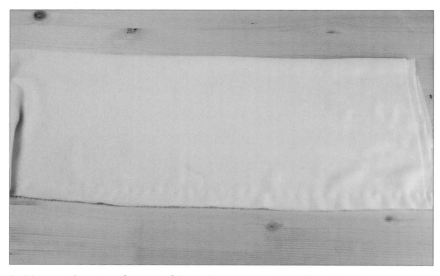

1. Measure the circumference of the pole you are using and cut the velvet to 4cm (1⅝in) wider for a seam allowance. Fold the velvet in half with the wrong sides together and tack along the join 2cm (¾in) from the edge to make a tube.

2. Pull the fabric tube over the pole. It should fit snugly.

3. Push the tube down the pole. This is easier if you are wearing rubber gloves, which grip well. Push the seam straight as you go.

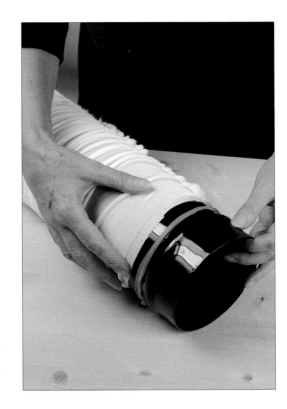

4. Wind several wide elastic bands round the end of the pole to prevent the fabric tube from slipping off.

5. Stand the pole upright and push the velvet tube down hard to push the fabric into pleats.

6. Continue until all the fabric is evenly compressed. Wind wide elastic bands round the pole at the top of the fabric.

7. Spray the fabric thoroughly with water to damp right into the folds and then compress it again, moving up the elastic bands to stop it slipping back.

8. Prepare blue, turquoise and viridian steam-fix dyes in a palette, diluting some shades with water to vary the tone. Place the pole in a plastic tray and use foam brushes to paint round the compressed fabric tube in rings. Apply the dyes generously so that they soak deep into the creases. Work each band into the previous colour to blend.

9. Leave the piece to dry horizontally across the tray in a warm place, turning it round from time to time so the dyes dry evenly. Check between the folds – when it is completely dry, it is ready for steaming.

10. Wrap the piece in newspaper to protect it from condensation and tape the edges with masking tape. Stand it on a trivet in a bucket of boiling water, filled to just below the trivet level so the wrapped velvet does not get splashed. Cover the top of the pole with foil.

11. Cover the pole and the top of the bucket with foil and pinch it together at the top and round the bucket rim to keep the steam in. Steam the piece for two hours, topping up with boiling water to just below the trivet as necessary.

12. Slide the steamed velvet off the pole and remove the tacking thread to open it up. Rinse it well in cold running water, then wash it in warm water and spin dry it. Tumble dry it for 10–15 minutes to bring up the pile, or line dry it.

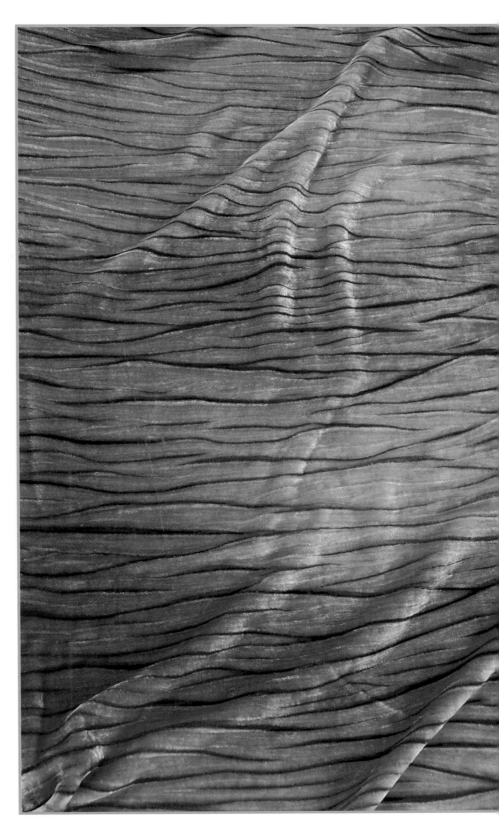

The finished piece, showing how the dye migrates to the top of the folds as the velvet dries, creating broken, wavy lines.

Pole-wrapped velvets. The navy and black scarf (top right) was dyed, then discharged to get light stripes on a darker background.

Pole wrapping, binding and pleating

In this pole wrapping project, space-dyed silk satin is over-dyed with black, but you could also use plain coloured silk and over-dye it in a different colour. The binding process takes a little practice – the thread must be kept tensioned or the pleats will slip, and it is important to compress the pleats tightly so that the dye can not penetrate too deeply into the folds. It is much easier to push the silk down in sections rather than trying to pleat the whole length in one go. Wrapping fabric diagonally around a long pole, then binding and pleating it is called 'arashi', which means 'storm' in Japanese, because the diagonal lines look like driving rain. If the fabric is folded in half or quarters before wrapping, as in this project, zigzag lines are created which resemble feathers.

You will need

A space-dyed silk scarf with pre-rolled edges, approx. 50cm (19¾in) wide x 152cm (60in) long
Iron
Wide elastic bands
Large pole
Strong thread and string
Masking tape
Black acid dye

1. Fold and iron the silk into four, lengthwise. Wind several wide elastic bands round the end of the pole and lay the silk at an angle, tucking a corner under the elastic bands to keep it in place.

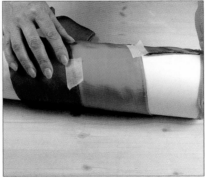

2. Wind the silk clockwise round the pole, butting up the edges but not overlapping them. Secure the silk temporarily with pieces of masking tape.

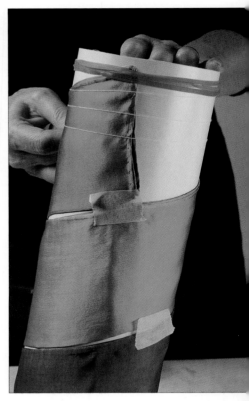

3. Tie strong thread to the elastic bands and stand the pole upright. Pull the thread to keep it tensioned as you turn the pole anti-clockwise so that the thread winds round the silk clockwise.

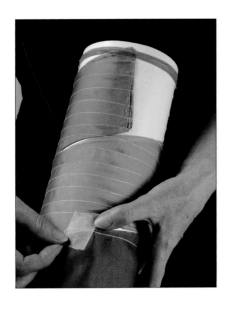

4. Continue winding, keeping the spacing of the threads even and removing the masking tape as you go. After binding about a 25cm (10in) section, secure the thread temporarily to the silk with masking tape to keep it tensioned and roughly wrap and secure the rest of the silk around the pole.

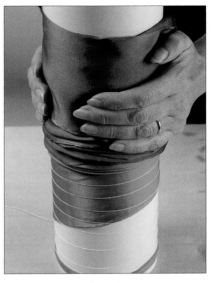

5. Turn the pole the other way up and, using both hands, carefully push down the silk without twisting to make smooth, even pleats.

6. Keep pushing down firmly and evenly until the whole thread-bound section is pleated.

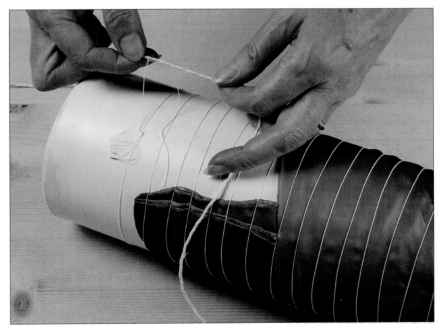

7. Lay the pole flat again, smooth out the next section and wrap it round the pole, securing with masking tape as before. Keep your thumb on the binding thread to keep it tensioned, remove the masking tape and continue binding. Repeat the process until the whole length is bound. Secure the thread temporarily with masking tape and tie the end to a piece of string.

8. Tie the string tightly round the pole to keep the thread tensioned. Remove the masking tape so that the silk can slide freely.

9. Push the silk down again to complete the pleating and tightly compress it.

10. Soak the piece well in a bucket of water. Mix a strong black dye bath, deep enough to immerse all the silk, and bring it to 80°C (176°F). Lower the silk in to the dye for a minute or so.

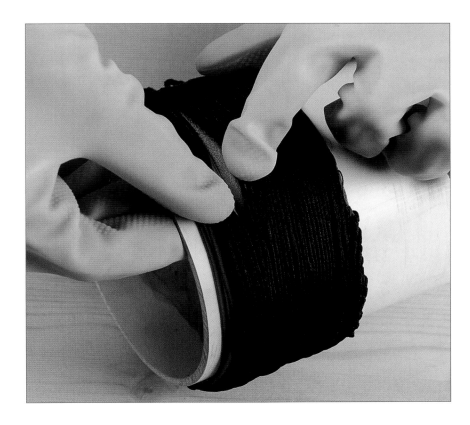

11. Rinse the piece and check between the folds to make sure the dye is not penetrating too far. Dip again if necessary to get a strong, even black across the surface of the pleats, then rinse well on the pole.

12. To retain the pleats, leave the silk on the pole in a warm place to dry thoroughly before unwrapping it.

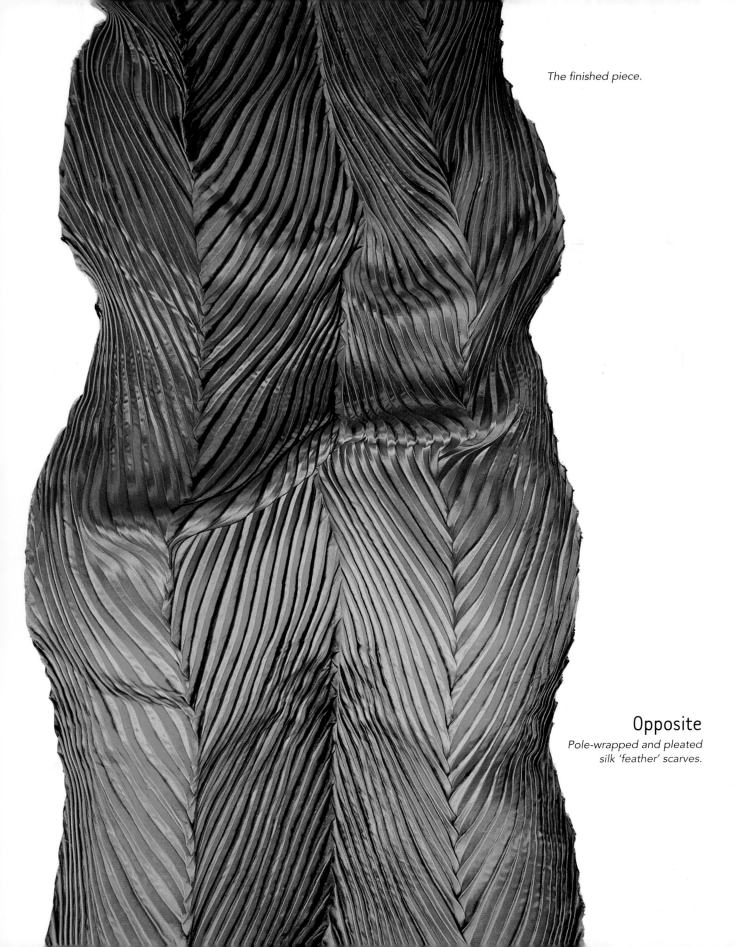

The finished piece.

Opposite

Pole-wrapped and pleated silk 'feather' scarves.

Index